4/17/12
$4.70

Tobacco and Smoking

Other Books of Related Interest:

Opposing Viewpoints Series

Addiction
Birth Defects
Health

Current Controversies Series

Health Care
Smoking

At Issue Series

Alcohol Abuse
Cancer
How Does Advertising Impact Teen Behavior?
Marijuana

> "Congress shall make no law … abridging the freedom of speech, or of the press."

First Amendment to the US Constitution

The basic foundation of our democracy is the First Amendment guarantee of freedom of expression. The Opposing Viewpoints Series is dedicated to the concept of this basic freedom and the idea that it is more important to practice it than to enshrine it.

OPPOSING
VIEWPOINTS®
SERIES

Tobacco and Smoking

Kelly Wand, Book Editor

GREENHAVEN PRESS
A part of Gale, Cengage Learning

GALE
CENGAGE Learning·

Detroit • New York • San Francisco • New Haven, Conn • Waterville, Maine • London

Elizabeth Des Chenes, *Managing Editor*

© 2012 Greenhaven Press, a part of Gale, Cengage Learning

Gale and Greenhaven Press are registered trademarks used herein under license.

For more information, contact:
Greenhaven Press
27500 Drake Rd.
Farmington Hills, MI 48331-3535
Or you can visit our Internet site at gale.cengage.com.

For product information and technology assistance, contact us at:

Gale Customer Support, 1-800-877-4253.
For permission to use material from this text or product, submit all requests online at www.cengage.com/permissions.

Further permissions questions can be emailed to permissionrequest@cengage.com.

Articles in Greenhaven Press anthologies are often edited for length to meet page requirements. In addition, original titles of these works are changed to clearly present the main thesis and to explicitly indicate the author's opinion. Every effort is made to ensure the Greenhaven Press accurately reflects the original intent of the authors. Every effort has been made to trace the owners of copyrighted material.

Cover Image © Tetra Images/Corbis.

LIBRARY OF CONGRESS CATALOGING-IN-PUBLICATION DATA

Tobacco and smoking / Kelly Wand, book editor.
    p. cm. -- (Opposing viewpoints)
    Summary: "Tobacco and Smoking: Is Tobacco Use A Serious Problem?; Should Tobacco Use Be Regulated?; Should Smoking Alternatives Be Regulated?; How Do the Media Affect Individuals' Choice to Smoke?"-- Provided by publisher.
    Includes bibliographical references and index.
    ISBN 978-0-7377-5909-9 (hardback) -- ISBN 978-0-7377-5910-5 (pbk.)
  1. Tobacco use--United States. 2. Smoking--United States. 3. Tobacco use.
  4. Smoking. I. Wand, Kelly.
    HV5760.T615 2012
    362.29'60973--dc23
                                                        2011038894

Printed in the United States of America
1 2 3 4 5 6 7 16 15 14 13 12

Contents

Chapter 3: Should Smoking Alternatives Be Regulated?

Chapter 4: How Do the Media Affect Individuals' Choice to Smoke?

Why Consider
Opposing Viewpoints?

> *"The only way in which a human being
> can make some approach to knowing
> the whole of a subject is by hearing
> what can be said about it by persons of
> every variety of opinion and studying
> all modes in which it can be looked at
> by every character of mind. No wise
> man ever acquired his wisdom in any
> mode but this."*
>
> *John Stuart Mill*

In our media-intensive culture it is not difficult to find differing opinions. Thousands of newspapers and magazines and dozens of radio and television talk shows resound with differing points of view. The difficulty lies in deciding which opinion to agree with and which "experts" seem the most credible. The more inundated we become with differing opinions and claims, the more essential it is to hone critical reading and thinking skills to evaluate these ideas. Opposing Viewpoints books address this problem directly by presenting stimulating debates that can be used to enhance and teach these skills. The varied opinions contained in each book examine many different aspects of a single issue. While examining these conveniently edited opposing views, readers can develop critical thinking skills such as the ability to compare and contrast authors' credibility, facts, argumentation styles, use of persuasive techniques, and other stylistic tools. In short, the Opposing Viewpoints Series is an ideal way to attain the higher-level thinking and reading skills so essential in a culture of diverse and contradictory opinions.

In addition to providing a tool for critical thinking, Opposing Viewpoints books challenge readers to question their own strongly held opinions and assumptions. Most people form their opinions on the basis of upbringing, peer pressure, and personal, cultural, or professional bias. By reading carefully balanced opposing views, readers must directly confront new ideas as well as the opinions of those with whom they disagree. This is not to argue simplistically that everyone who reads opposing views will—or should—change his or her opinion. Instead, the series enhances readers' understanding of their own views by encouraging confrontation with opposing ideas. Careful examination of others' views can lead to the readers' understanding of the logical inconsistencies in their own opinions, perspective on why they hold an opinion, and the consideration of the possibility that their opinion requires further evaluation.

Evaluating Other Opinions

To ensure that this type of examination occurs, Opposing Viewpoints books present all types of opinions. Prominent spokespeople on different sides of each issue as well as well-known professionals from many disciplines challenge the reader. An additional goal of the series is to provide a forum for other, less known, or even unpopular viewpoints. The opinion of an ordinary person who has had to make the decision to cut off life support from a terminally ill relative, for example, may be just as valuable and provide just as much insight as a medical ethicist's professional opinion. The editors have two additional purposes in including these less known views. One, the editors encourage readers to respect others' opinions—even when not enhanced by professional credibility. It is only by reading or listening to and objectively evaluating others' ideas that one can determine whether they are worthy of consideration. Two, the inclusion of such viewpoints encourages the important critical thinking skill of objectively evaluating an author's credentials and bias. This evaluation will illuminate an author's reasons for taking a particular stance on an issue and will aid in readers' evaluation of the author's ideas.

It is our hope that these books will give readers a deeper understanding of the issues debated and an appreciation of the complexity of even seemingly simple issues when good and honest people disagree. This awareness is particularly important in a democratic society such as ours in which people enter into public debate to determine the common good. Those with whom one disagrees should not be regarded as enemies but rather as people whose views deserve careful examination and may shed light on one's own.

Thomas Jefferson once said that "difference of opinion leads to inquiry, and inquiry to truth." Jefferson, a broadly educated man, argued that "if a nation expects to be ignorant and free . . . it expects what never was and never will be." As individuals and as a nation, it is imperative that we consider the opinions of others and examine them with skill and discernment. The Opposing Viewpoints Series is intended to help readers achieve this goal.

David L. Bender and Bruno Leone,
Founders

Introduction

> "If an addict who has been completely
> cured starts smoking again, he no
> longer experiences the discomfort of his
> first addiction. There exists, therefore,
> outside alkaloids and habit, a sense
> for opium, an intangible habit, which
> lives on, despite the recasting of the
> organism. The dead drug leaves a ghost
> behind. At certain hours it haunts the
> house."
>
> Jean Cocteau, artist (1889–1963)

Inhaling the smoke of dried leaves has been a human custom for thousands of years. Although definitive records of cannabis smoking date back to the early Bronze Age, many ancient cultures, including the Egyptians and the Romans, cultivated poppies for opium used in the production of food and anesthesia, as well as a central component of various ceremonial rituals. By comparison, there is no written record of tobacco being used recreationally until French and Spanish explorers of the fifteenth century co-opted the practice from indigenous tribes in the New World and brought it back with them. While it was initially (and somewhat ironically) regarded as a benign herbal medicine when presented to the French court of Catherine de Medici in 1559 by French diplomat Jean Nicot (from whose name the word "nicotine" is derived), tobacco's use as a symbol and instrument of leisure spread rapidly throughout Europe.

The first citywide smoking bans sprang up within the next few decades, at first in Bavaria and Austria, but were for the most part poorly enforced. Pope Urban VII, whose inauspicious reign lasted a mere thirteen days before malaria claimed his life, would nevertheless be immortalized for his proclamation of the first written (and until then most rigorous) smoking ban on record, when in A.D. 1590 he warned that anyone who "took tobacco in the porchway of or inside a church, whether it be by chewing it, smoking it with a pipe, or sniffing it in powdered form through the nose" would be excommunicated. The first national smoking ban came about more than 350 years later when in the twentieth century a zero tolerance tobacco moratorium was declared in every university, post office, military hospital, and Party office, all to be scrupulously overseen by the Institute for Tobacco Hazards Research. The country was Germany, the campaign's organizer: Adolf Hitler.

There was little organized effort to research smoking's side effects outside of Germany until after World War II, because of the limitations of existing technology to study its effects and a predisposition for optimism, even by the most hard-hearted members of the scientific community. The Nobel Prize-winning scientist Marie Curie once marveled fearlessly at the pretty blue-green elfin light that the test tubes of radioactive isotopes she carried in her pocket and stored in her desk drawers emanated, little suspecting the catastrophic radioactivity to which she was obliviously exposing herself. Similarly, the notion that something as innocuous, small, and mood enhancing as a cigarette or cigar could be toxic to the lungs of the user, let alone those around her, seemed preposterous. When British physiologist Richard Doll first undertook his study of lung cancer patients in 1950, even he fully expected to learn that the origin was either automobile fumes or the increasingly ubiquitous road surface known as tarmac. He found instead that the only factor every patient logged in twenty London hospitals had in common was tobacco smoking. Though his findings were published in the *British Medical Journal* a few months later and convinced Doll himself to stop smoking, nearly forty years would pass before the four rich and powerful corporations comprising the United States tobacco industry conceded in a landmark agreement with the federal government that it was in any way, shape, or form guilty of marketing a product that killed people.

Smoke and Mirrors

In the years following the surgeon general's 1964 proclamation, based on more than seven thousand scientific articles (including Doll's), that tobacco use caused cancer, tobacco manufacturers consistently responded by mounting advertising campaigns that internal documents would later reveal were deliberately targeted at adolescents. In response to the growing number of anti-tobacco groups lobbying for stricter policing of tobacco sales to the youth market, the companies founded organizations of their own with names such as the Center for Indoor Air Research and the Tobacco Institute. Though their findings were cloaked in scientific jargon, the purpose of these think tanks was simple: to attack, or at least cast doubt on, scientific studies that confirmed the health hazards of tobacco, as well as to provide lobbyists who would implore, or bribe, politicians to ease or end tobacco restrictions of any kind.

Yet as the mortality statistics continued to pile up, the antismoking movement gained momentum and credibility. By 1998, pressure on US tobacco companies reached a fever pitch. Class-action lawsuits filed by more than eight hundred individuals and more than forty attorney generals alleged that in contributing to health problems among the population and consequent medical costs incurred by the public health system, the tobacco companies were in violation of numerous consumer-protection laws.

In 1997, R.J. Reynolds caved to pressure over a lawsuit broached by San Francisco attorney Janet Mangini and voluntarily replaced its decade-long advertising cartoonish mascot Joe Camel with a non-anthropomorphic quadruped. A year later, in September 1998, the four largest tobacco companies signed the Tobacco Master Settlement Agreement (MSA), in which they agreed to phase out marketing gimmicks aimed at adolescents, dissolve their lobbyist-spawning pools, and fund their own above-the-board antismoking group. There was also one final stipulation of note: The tobacco companies would also compensate the states directly in the amount of $206 billion over the next twenty-five years, purportedly to help recoup those medical costs and lost production hours by the deceased smokers.

While antismoking activists were satisfied by the reluctance and bitterness with which these sanctions were opposed by the tobacco industry and agreed that the resulting revenues would be put to far better use going towards maintaining infrastructure than simply lining the coffers of cigarette company tycoons, cynics noted that politicians demanding a cut of the action rather than effectively banning or restricting the sale of hazardous products hardly amounted to an act of altruism. Phase II of the settlement the following year also saw cigarette companies paying tobacco growers for their potential losses as the result of the higher cigarette prices the companies instated to cover the settlement's original costs. Yet another controversial aspect of the legislation involved charging subsequent "participating manufacturers" "buy-in fees" of market share costs that few smaller companies could ever afford, effectively giving the four big corporations a government-sponsored monopoly.

In the immediate wake of these measures, cigarette consumption dropped to a fifty-year low in 2004, but many antismoking advocates still perceived the MSA as, at best, a "lost opportunity to curb cigarette use" and questioned just how much of the settlement money was even being spent on tobacco reduction as called for in the legislation. Though the agreement was heralded by its authors as a "crackdown" on purveyors of a poisonous product, everyone was making more money off its continued distribution.

Everyone, at least, except the smokers.

To Smoke or Not to Smoke

There is little debate that smoking has caused a vast number of deaths and continues to exact a heavy toll every year in terms of human suffering. The World Health Organization estimates that smoking deaths worldwide will rise from 5.4 million deaths a year to 6.5 million in 2015 and 8.3 million by 2030 even if the most draconian antismoking measures currently under consideration are uniformly adopted. Data from the Centers for Disease Control and Prevention show that smoking-related deaths also cost the nation $92 billion a year in lost productivity and $75.5 billion in health costs. Such figures do not include the deaths and illness caused by smokeless tobacco and flavored cigarettes or the effects of secondhand smoke.

Yet as the moral and legal complexities of the MSA and other landmark litigation battles involving tobacco companies underscore, restricting a legal, portable, and profitable product that people choose to use regardless of the health consequences to themselves and those around them entails confronting further questions of even greater nuance. While nonsmokers complain that the pernicious residue of smoking affects them as well, smokers argue that their own quality of life is unreasonably impaired by antismoking regulations. They counter that many comforts we take for granted, such as electricity and automobiles, magnify air pollution, which harms the quality of life for the international community, yet few people seriously propose the abolition of electrical devices or a global reversion to horseback riding. Is targeting tobacco an effort to manage a public heath concern, or is it merely a convenient, easily demonized substitute for far graver problems too deeply ingrained to address?

In the chapters that follow, the viewpoint authors examine not just the extent to which big business and legislators can or should profit from products hazardous to people's health, but whether the rights of smokers and nonsmokers can coexist at all.

CHAPTER 1

Is Tobacco Use a Serious Problem?

Chapter Preface

According to a 2008 report issued by the World Health Organization (WHO), tobacco use was responsible for killing close to 100 million people over the course of the twentieth century, an estimate making it twice as deadly as the number of casualties worldwide attributed to World War II and roughly equivalent to those caused by the Black Death pandemic that in a single decade reduced the population of Europe to levels from which it would take nearly two hundred years to recover.

In its report, the WHO strongly urged members of the international community to adopt six policies of tobacco control it considered equally paramount: raising taxes and the price of tobacco products; banning tobacco advertising, sponsorship, and promotion; passing and enforcing far stricter regulations on secondhand smoke than any that had yet been imposed; warning the public about the dangers posed by tobacco; helping existing smokers in their efforts to quit; and refining the study of tobacco use and its effects in much greater detail in order to slow down and eventually reverse the epidemic.

Should such measures not be universally adopted in the immediate future, the report projected that the number of tobacco deaths for the twenty-first century would exceed 1 billion, or roughly the entire world population at the time of the American Revolution, eighty percent of them citizens of low or middle income. The figures left out the millions of lost work hours of productivity, all nonfatal medical ailments caused directly by tobacco use or indirectly by secondhand smoke, the consequences of diverting the resources of already overstrained health care institutions to treat the victims of smoking, not to mention the considerable and irreversible environmental issues resulting from discarded tobacco products and their manufacture.

In the face of such evidence, some would argue an immediate and permanent worldwide ban on all tobacco use, merely on the grounds of preserving human life, would not appear entirely unreasonable. Yet even the World Health Organization's report failed to cite an all-encompassing ban as one of its goals, even though it would surely be more effective than the implementation of all six of its policy proposals combined. One major reason such a far-reaching prohibition fails to even merit debate is simply recognition that, unlike those killed by the Black Death, tobacco's victims are, secondhand smoke notwithstanding, voluntary sufferers. The majority of the world's current smokers, even ones without access to detailed medical information or in nations where graphic warnings are not required on cigarette packs, are already fairly educated about the harms to which they are willingly subjecting themselves, and they choose to smoke anyway. Although many reports suggest that little of the tax money from American tobacco sales is used to actually subsidize the antismoking education for which it is intended, it has funded many projects and programs beneficial to the public. Over the advice of their spouses and physicians, numerous respected artists and intellectuals ranging from William Faulkner to Albert Einstein arguably have produced famous, even timeless contributions to human knowledge and culture either arguably while smoking or waiting to smoke. Some anthropologists would argue that tobacco deaths also serve as a morbid but effective means of population control.

The following viewpoints in this chapter will examine how serious the threat of tobacco is depending on what factors are being considered and who is doing the measuring, as well as whether any amount of regulation or education can be sufficient to curb an impulse cultivated and institutionalized across many cultures for a period of time that dates back long before smoking mortality rates were first recorded.

*"Despite significant declines during
the past 30 years, cigarette smoking
in the United States continues to be
widespread."*

Tobacco Use Is on the Rise

**S.R. Dube, A. McClave, C. James, R. Caraballo,
R. Kaufmann, and T. Pechacek**

*The authors are researchers at the Centers for Disease Control and
Prevention (CDC). In the following viewpoint, a weekly bulletin
issued by the Centers for Disease Control and Prevention, the authors describe the results of a nationwide survey that found cigarette smoking rising in every demographic. Though the evidence
they cite suggests that tobacco use is higher in certain groups, such
as those living near the poverty line, smoking overall is on the rise
regardless of race, age, or gender.*

As you read, consider the following questions:

1. According to the authors, what variations in smoking
   prevalence were observed in the survey results?
2. In the authors' view, why is youth smoking "an important
   indicator to monitor"?
3. What are two of the evidence-based strategies the authors

claim would be effective in reducing the prevalence of cigarette smoking for the entire population?

Cigarette smoking continues to be the leading cause of preventable morbidity and mortality in the United States. The negative health consequences of cigarette smoking have been well-documented and include cardiovascular disease, multiple cancers, pulmonary disease, adverse reproductive outcomes, and exacerbation of other chronic health conditions. Cigarette smoking causes approximately 443,000 premature deaths in the United States annually and $193 billion in direct health-care expenditures and productivity losses because of premature mortality each year.

Despite significant declines during the past 30 years, cigarette smoking in the United States continues to be widespread; in 2008, one in five U.S. adults (20.6%) were current smokers. Year-to-year decreases in smoking prevalence have been observed only sporadically in recent years. For example, a slight decrease occurred from 2006 to 2007 but not from 2007 to 2008. Monitoring tobacco use is essential in the effort to curb the epidemic of tobacco use. To assess progress toward the Healthy People 2010 objective of reducing the prevalence of cigarette smoking among adults to ≤ 12% (objective 27-1a), this report provides the most recent national estimates of smoking prevalence among adults aged ≥ 18 years, based on data from the 2009 National Health Interview Survey (NHIS), and provides state-level estimates based on data from the 2009 Behavioral Risk Factor Surveillance System (BRFSS) survey. . . .

Results of the Survey

In 2009, an estimated 20.6% (46.6 million) of U.S. adults were current cigarette smokers; of these, 78.1% (36.4 million) smoked every day, and 21.9% (10.2 million) smoked on some days. Prevalence of current smoking was higher among men (23.5%) than women (17.9%). Among racial/ethnic groups, Asians had the lowest prevalence (12.0%), and Hispanics had a lower prevalence of smoking (14.5%) than non-Hispanic blacks (21.3%) and non-Hispanic whites (22.1%). Adults reporting multiple races had the highest prevalence (29.5%), followed by American Indians/Alaska Natives (23.2%).

Variations in smoking prevalence in 2009 were observed by education level. Smoking prevalence was highest among adults who had obtained a General Education Development certificate (GED) (49.1%) and generally declined with increasing education, being lowest among adults with a graduate degree (5.6%). The prevalence of current smoking was higher among adults living below the federal poverty level (31.1%) than among those at or above this level (19.4%). Smoking prevalence did not vary significantly for adults aged 18–24 years (21.8%), 25–44 years (24.0%), and 45–64 years (21.9%); however, it was lowest for adults aged ≥ 65 years (9.5%). Regionally, smoking prevalence was higher in the Midwest (23.1%) and South (21.8%), and lowest prevalence for adult current smoking was observed for the West (16.4%).

During 2005–2009, the proportion of U.S. adults who were current cigarette smokers was 20.9% in 2005 and 20.6% in 2009, with no significant difference. No significant changes in current smoking prevalence for U.S. adults were observed during the 5-year period overall and for each of the four regions: Northeast, Midwest, South, or West.

By state, the prevalence of current smoking ranged from 9.8% (Utah) to 25.6% (Kentucky and West Virginia). States with the highest prevalence of adult current smoking were clustered in the Midwest and Southeast regions.

Conclusions and Comment

The results of these analyses indicate that the national estimates for the prevalence of current cigarette smoking among adults aged ≥ 18 years did not decline from 2008 (20.6%) to 2009, and during the past 5 years (2005–2009) virtually no change has been observed, even by region. In 2009, certain population subgroups

Percentage of Smokers Age 18 and Older by State, 2009

Persons who reported smoking at least 100 cigarettes during their lifetime and who, at the time of the survey, reported smoking every day or some days.

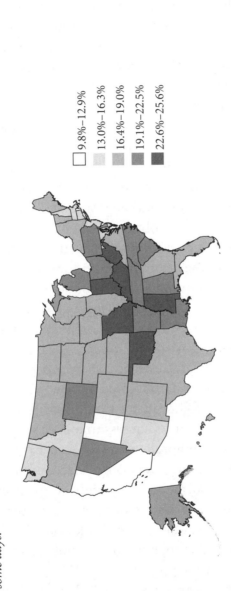

9.8%–12.9%

13.0%–16.3%

16.4%–19.0%

19.1%–22.5%

22.6%–25.6%

The figure above shows the percentage of persons age ≥18 years, by state, who were current cigarette smokers in the United States in 2009, based on data from the Behavioral Risk Factor Surveillance System. The prevalence of current smoking ranged from 9.8% (Utah) to 25.6% (Kentucky and West Virginia). States with the highest prevalence of adult current smoking were clustered in the Midwest and Southeast regions.

TAKEN FROM: *Morbidity and Mortality Weekly Report,* vol. 59, no. 35, p. 1138.

(e.g., Hispanic and Asian women, persons with higher levels of education, and older adults) continue to meet the Healthy People 2010 target of ≤ 12% prevalence of smoking. Although smoking prevalence was found to be lowest among Asian and Hispanic women, the findings in this report cannot assess specific Asian and Hispanic subgroups. In a previous report, variations in smoking prevalence were observed within specific Asian and Hispanic subgroups and between the sexes within these subgroups, suggesting that overall prevalence for Asians and Hispanics do not accurately represent the wide variability across subgroups.

Differences in understanding the health hazards of smoking and receptivity to anti-smoking messages might be related to the prevalence variations observed by education level. For example, persons with higher levels of education might have a better understanding of the health hazards of smoking and might be more receptive to health messaging about the dangers of smoking. Nonetheless, most population subgroups, particularly those with low education and income levels, will not meet the Healthy People 2010 target.

Differences also were noted by state and region. In 2009, the lowest prevalence was observed in the West, with lowest prevalence in Utah, followed by California. California traditionally has been cited for its success in tobacco control because of its long-running comprehensive tobacco control program. California's adult smoking prevalence declined approximately 40% during 1998–2006, and consequently lung cancer incidence in California has been declining four times faster than in the rest of the nation. Similarly, Maine, New York, and Washington have seen 45%–60% in reductions in youth smoking with sustained comprehensive statewide programs.

Youth smoking is an important indicator to monitor because most adult established smokers (>80%) begin before the age of 18 years. In 2009, one in five U.S. high school students (19.5%) reported smoking cigarettes in the preceding 30 days. Moreover, declines in current smoking among high school students have slowed, with an 11% decline from 21.9% in 2003 to 19.5% in 2009 compared with a 40% decline observed from 1997 (36.4%) to 2003 (21.9%). The slowing in the decline observed for youth cigarette smoking indicates that cigarette smoking among adults and the associated morbidity and mortality will continue to be important public health issues for the foreseeable future. . . .

The Healthy People 2010 objective of reducing the overall prevalence of cigarette smoking among U.S. adults to ≤ 12% will not be met in 2010. However, for some subpopulations and states, this goal has been reached, demonstrating that the national target is achievable. To meet this goal for the entire population in the future, evidence-based strategies focused on populations such as persons with lower education are needed. Effective strategies including price increases, comprehensive smoke-free policies, and media campaigns to counter pro-tobacco industry influences need to be implemented aggressively in coordination with providing access to affordable and effective cessation treatments and services. If each state sustained comprehensive tobacco control programs for 5 years with CDC-recommended levels of funding, an estimated 5 million fewer persons in the country would smoke, resulting in prevention of premature tobacco-related deaths. . . .

Key Points

- Smoking causes approximately 443,000 premature deaths, accounts for up to 30% of cancer deaths, and is the single most preventable cause of disease and death in the United States.
- Despite the adverse health effects of smoking cigarettes, one in five U.S. adults (46.6 million men and women) currently smoke.
- The prevalence of adult smoking is not decreasing. Effective population-based strategies to encourage cessation

(e.g., tobacco taxes, smoke-free policies, and media campaigns) are essential to accelerate the reduction in tobacco use among adults in the United States and prevent smoking initiation in young persons.

| "*What we have is an enormous social change in terms of what is considered acceptable behavior.*"

Tobacco Use Is Decreasing

Marc Kaufman

Marc Kaufman is a reporter for the Washington Post. *In this viewpoint, he claims that overall, smoking in the United States has been in steady decline since 1951. Among the main reasons for this decline, Kaufman cites the rising prices of cigarettes, as well as the increasing difficulties that smokers face in the forms of social stigma and smoking bans in public areas and the workplace.*

As you read, consider the following questions:
1. According to the author, what are three reasons that tobacco-control advocates cite for the drop in smoking across the United States?
2. In the author's view, how have tobacco companies offset their legal costs over cigarette-related lawsuits?
3. What does the author claim is the financial downside of the decline in smoking for some states?

A mericans smoked fewer cigarettes last year [in 2005] than at any time since 1951, and the nation's per capita consumption of tobacco fell to levels not seen since the early 1930s, the association of state attorneys general reported yesterday.

Using data the federal government gathers when it collects taxes on cigarette sales, the group found a 4.2 percent decline in 2005 alone and an overall drop of more than 20 percent since tobacco companies reached a legal settlement with the states in 1998.

Association leaders and other tobacco-control advocates hailed the decline as a sign that sometimes-controversial developments triggered by the $246 billion settlement have been effective. The drop was a result, they said, of factors that include the sharply higher cost of cigarettes, restrictions on cigarette advertising and a shift in public perceptions as the dangers of smoking are more aggressively and widely publicized.

"I think we're reaching a tipping point, where the image of tobacco is that it's unhealthy and dangerous, and not glamorous like years ago or neutral like the cigarette companies say now," said Tom Miller, Iowa's attorney general and co-chairman of the National Association of Attorneys General's tobacco committee.

"We've seen a big drop in cigarette smoking, but I think we can still cut the smoking rate substantially more," he said.

"One Battle We're Winning"

Cheryl Healton, president of the American Legacy Foundation, a tobacco-control group initially funded by the legal settlement, said the continuing decline suggests that the national health goal of reducing smoking rates even further . . . is within reach.

"We're on target to exceed the national goal" of having no more than 15 percent of youths and 12 percent of adults smoking, Healton said. Few of the other national health goals adopted in 2000 appear to be achievable, she said, "but this is one battle we're winning."

Federal studies show that about 21.7 percent of high school students still smoke, as do 20.9 percent of adults—about 45 million Americans 18 and older. Tobacco use remains the leading preventable cause of death, causing more than 400,000 deaths a year.

The decline in smoking began more than 20 years ago but accelerated after the settlement. Healton said the drop is a result of fewer people starting the habit, more people quitting and many cutting back on the number of cigarettes they smoke.

Some of those trends were unrelated to the settlement, such as the decisions by 12 states, the District, Puerto Rico, and hundreds of cities and counties to ban smoking in public buildings, including restaurants and bars. "With all the restrictions in place now on smoking in public areas, it's just difficult to smoke as much as before," Healton said.

She said the sharp increase in the price of cigarettes since the settlement—from an average of $ 1.74 a pack in 1997 to $3.16 in 2004—has been especially important in reducing the number of young people who start smoking.

Michael Neese, spokesman for Philip Morris USA, said the company has always expected that the settlement would bring about "meaningful change." A call to R.J. Reynolds Tobacco Co. was not returned.

Where the Money Goes

The association's study found that about 378 billion cigarettes were sold in the United States last year—the lowest number since 1951, when the population was half of what it is today. Although the official 2005 total did not take into account growing but untraceable Internet sales and other black-market supplies, officials said those sources remain miniscule compared with legal purchases.

The heart of the agreement reached between the states and the tobacco industry in 1998 is the $246 billion being paid to settle lawsuits over cigarette-related health costs. Tobacco companies

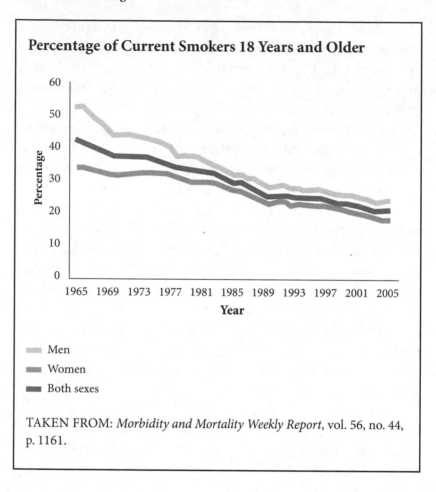

Percentage of Current Smokers 18 Years and Older

Men

Women

Both sexes

TAKEN FROM: *Morbidity and Mortality Weekly Report*, vol. 56, no. 44, p. 1161.

generally passed their costs along in the form of higher prices, which in turn reduced cigarette sales.

But Miller and other tobacco-control advocates said yesterday that the agreement has also helped change the public's view of smoking. With the banning of ads such as those featuring the character "Joe Camel" and the expansion of aggressive anti-smoking ad campaigns, they said, the message that many young people are getting is dramatically different from the one of 10 years ago, when teenage smoking was on the rise.

"The long-term trend is perfectly clear and consistent," said Mark Greenwald, director of the Tobacco Project for the association of state attorneys general. "What we have is an enormous social change in terms of what is considered acceptable behavior."

The Downside of Declining Cigarette Sales

Although the steep decline in cigarette sales has been a public health boon, it has become something of a financial problem for some states. Because industry payments to states are based to some extent on the number of cigarettes sold, the settlement revenue has dropped.

The 46 states that signed the settlement initially expected about $6.5 billion this spring, for instance, but the tobacco companies have said that they may be entitled to cut the payments by as much as $1.2 billion this year. Some of that decline would be the result of dropping sales, and some could come from other adjustments allowed under the settlement.

In particular, the major tobacco companies have said, the agreement allows them to reduce payments if their collective market share falls below a certain threshold—something they say occurred in 2003 after a substantial number of Americans switched to low-cost generic cigarettes. The states disputed that interpretation, and the issue is in arbitration.

But Iowa's Miller said states are ready for reductions in tobacco payments that are based on declining sales, and even welcome them.

"We knew from the beginning that if we succeeded in changing the cigarette culture, that sales would drop and so would our payments," he said. "But states deal with rising and declining revenues all the time, and this is one decline we're quite happy to see."

> *"I didn't think it was a big deal to have one at first, and then three or four at a party."*

Teenage Social Smoking Leads to Nicotine Addiction

Richa Gulati

Richa Gulati is a writer based in New York City. In the following viewpoint, Gulati interviews teenagers who admit that becoming addicted to cigarettes was a direct result of what began as enjoying an occasional smoke at parties with friends. Health experts that Gulati quotes claim such stories are not uncommon and that not only does non-daily use often result in nicotine dependence, but due to their brain chemistry, youths are more susceptible to such addictions than any other demographic.

As you read, consider the following questions:

1. According to Dr. Mark Rubinstein, why is infrequent smoking hazardous for teenagers?
2. In the author's view, what makes the nicotine patch an ineffectual means of quitting smoking for teenagers?
3. What are two methods the author claims can help teen smokers quit?

The first time I smoked was at a party when I was fourteen. A group of older kids were doing it, and they offered me a cigarette. I wanted to fit in and look cool, so I tried it," says Chantal, now seventeen. She thought it seemed relaxing—she continued to smoke with friends after school or out at night but never did it alone, so she figured her cigarette use was under control. "I was naïve," she admits. "I didn't think it was a big deal to have one at first, and then three or four at a party. But before I knew it, I was smoking every week and I started to feel like I needed a cigarette."

Cancer, heart disease, emphysema: The list of smoking's potential hazards is lengthy and exhaustively reported. Yet, according to the Centers for Disease Control and Prevention, nearly a quarter of all high school students across the country still smoke. Chances are, they got hooked because of social smoking. "Nearly two-thirds of current smokers became addicted to cigarettes during social smoking," says Joseph DiFranza, M.D., a family-medicine physician at the University of Massachusetts at Worcester Medical Center and an author of a study on adolescents and social smoking, which shows that—contrary to popular belief—non-daily tobacco use does trigger nicotine dependence. And, scarily enough, young people are the group most at risk. "Teens think that if you don't light up daily, you can't get addicted," DiFranza explains.

But it's a vicious cycle: even minimal exposure to nicotine can create cravings that escalate cigarette use, which in turn causes stronger cravings and withdrawal symptoms. "You can get hooked on even a few cigarettes a month," DiFranza notes. "Plus, smoking has cumulative effects—every cigarette increases the risk of addiction even if time lapses in between each one."

How can such infrequent smoking be so hazardous? "Nicotine fundamentally changes the brain," says Mark Rubinstein, M.D., a professor at the University of California at San Francisco Medical Center. "It's believed that the neural connections needed to create a new addiction can develop more easily in a young, growing teenage brain compared with an adult brain." DiFranza adds, "Just as a teenager can learn a language or how to use a gadget faster than an adult can, the teenage brain can 'learn' to get hooked on nicotine faster than an adult's can—and the addiction is stronger."

"There's a significant difference in the likelihood of lifetime addiction and ability to quit between, for example, someone who tries their first cigarettes in their 20s and someone who begins in their teens," Rubinstein explains. His research corroborates that the younger you start, the harder it is to quit—and the youngest smokers are the most at risk for being unable to ever stop. "I don't like the term social smoking because it makes the habit seem innocuous and controllable or even OK if it's done with others. But the reality is, teen social smoking is a high-risk activity," Rubinstein says.

Anne,* seventeen, from New York City, agrees. "I always thought that I never had to smoke at parties—I chose to—and that I could say no anytime," she says. "I just never actually turned it down." But at some point, she stopped smoking only with friends and started to turn to cigarettes when she was stressed. She then realized it might be more than a social habit—and that it was getting increasingly hard to say no.

Recognizing she may have had a smoking problem, however, didn't make it easy to stop. Like Anne, Chantal had a hard time quitting, which doesn't surprise Clea McNeely, a professor at the University of Tennessee at Knoxville who studies the social aspects of adolescent health. "Not only do teens not realize that they can become addicted to cigarettes by smoking even infrequently, but compared with adults, they face a significant challenge in quitting," McNeely explains. "Because cigarettes are so powerfully addictive for teens, it's hard for them to quit smoking even if they are not smoking daily. Nearly 81 percent of teens fail to stop on their first attempt," DiFranza says.

Common methods like nicotine patches, sprays, and medications used to treat adult smoking addiction haven't proven effective in treating teens. For example, because teens can be physically dependent on nicotine at such low levels of exposure, the patch (whose dosage was created to treat adults) often delivers too high a dose of nicotine, rendering it useless for many adolescent light smokers. With a lack of good options available, how can teens quit? Cessation therapy along with medical guidance can help. Both Anne and Chantal found support groups that guided them through the cessation process. (Chantal worked with a counselor through the Campaign for Tobacco-Free Kids.)

The research collected by groups like these may be also helpful in understanding why teens smoke in the first place. As McNeely stresses, parents who smoke are the biggest predictor for whether teens smoke; stress, poor body image, and desire to fit in are strong risk factors too. These underlying motivations often need to be addressed to truly change teen smoking habits. "Smoking not only made me feel relaxed physically but also attractive socially," admits Anne, whose habit escalated from a few cigarettes a month to nearly a pack and a half a week. "But going through cessation therapy made me realize that cigarettes masked my low self-esteem."

Ultimately, in order to quit, both Anne and Chantal had to change their social circles to limit the tempting places that might trigger a desire to light up. "I stopped hanging out with kids who smoked and avoided going to parties and places where I knew I would want to smoke or where someone else would encourage me," Anne says. Chantal adds: "These days I see smoking as ugly. I feel more in control of my future since I've kicked it. And I'm happier and healthier being around friends who don't push bad habits. Today, when other teens say that smoking looks cool or makes them feel calm, I tell them to try the gym, meditation, or even a new dress if you want to look better—just not a cigarette. There are a million ways to be more attractive other than by slowly killing yourself."

* Name has been changed.

*"Lower rates of smoking among black
teens may be the result of black parents
setting concrete guidelines about
substance use."*

Social Smoking Demographics

NewsRX Science

NewsRx Science is a weekly newsletter on recent results from scientific research in the United States. In the following viewpoint, a study reveals that fewer black teens smoke than white teens. The authors believe that parents have a strong influence over teens and their smoking behaviors. The viewpoint contends that by parents talking with their teens about smoking and other pressures, they can prevent substance abuse later in life.

As you read, consider the following questions:

1. At what age do most smokers begin smoking?
2. According to the article, does associating with teens who smoke make others more likely to smoke?

It's a curious paradox. Black adults are more likely to smoke than white adults and most smokers start as teenagers. But statistics show that fewer black youths than whites begin smoking as adolescents.

A new University of Washington [UW] study indicates that lower rates of smoking among black teens may be the result of black parents setting concrete guidelines about substance use and establishing clearly defined consequences for not following those guidelines.

The research also found that teens who associated with deviant peers—those who were in trouble at school, or who engaged in delinquent behavior or used alcohol or marijuana—were more likely to smoke, according to Martie Skinner, a research scientist with the Social Development Research Group, part of the UW's School of Social Work and the study's lead author.

"This study is important because we looked at how parental guidelines affected peer influences and smoking over a three-year period from the eighth to 10th grades," she said. "Parents can have a strong influence on smoking behavior.

"In general, good parenting such as setting clear guidelines about drug use and forming strong relationships with your child reduces the likelihood of teens associating with deviant peers and has a significant impact on whether kids smoke or don't smoke. Our findings are consistent with other research done here which shows parents are important influences on their teenagers including who they should hang out with.

Peers and Smoking

"Associating with other teens using substances increases a teen's chances of using those substances. This applied to both black and white teens. The majority of eighth graders don't use substances, so it is easy to find other peers who don't use them," she said.

The study found that 15 percent of the black teens reported smoking in the 10th grade compared to 22 percent of the white teens. Black parents were significantly more likely to report guidelines and consequences for substance use. Not surprisingly, black and white teens whose parents smoked reported higher levels of smoking than teens whose parents were non-smokers.

Skinner and her Social Development Research Group colleagues Kevin Haggerty and Richard Catalano collected data from a larger Seattle study designed to prevent substance abuse. The smoking study looked at 331 families—163 black and 168 white—with slightly more boys than girls.

Skinner thinks rates of smoking among blacks accelerate after leaving high school, a time when many black adolescents are not going to college and move away from their parents' home. She is following the same pool of teenagers in this study to assess their levels of smoking in a follow-up project.

So what can parents do to discourage teen smoking and other substance use? Skinner suggests:

- talking about smoking and substance use directly and not ignoring the topic.
- establishing family guidelines about smoking and moderate consequences for breaking those guidelines.
- keeping communication open so you know what your teen is doing and to maintain a strong relationship.

"These things can be hard to do in the real heat of life," Skinner said. "Getting support from other adults in the child's life, such as teachers, is key. Parenting is the most important thing we do, so we shouldn't hesitate to get help.

"We know family-based interventions can be effective and specific skills to promote healthy development in teens are pretty easily acquired if parents are given good instruction."

| "*Exposure to second-hand smoke is still one of the most common indoor pollutants worldwide.*"

Secondhand Smoke Negatively Impacts People Worldwide

Mattias Oberg, Maritta S. Jaakkola, Alistair Woodward, Armando Peruga, and Annette Pruss-Ustun

Mattias Oberg is a researcher at the Karolinska Institute in Stockholm, Sweden; Maritta S. Jaakkola is a professor at the University of Oulu in Finland; Alistair Woodward is a professor at New Zealand's University of Auckland; and Armando Peruga and Annette Pruss-Ustun are scholars at the World Health Organization in Geneva, Switzerland. In the following viewpoint, the authors describe the results of a study on the effects of secondhand smoke in data compiled from 192 countries. They conclude that not only is exposure to secondhand smoke much more pervasive than previous estimates have suggested, but that the number of deaths and diseases caused by secondhand smoke is also far higher than the general public is aware of, especially among women and young children.

As you read, consider the following questions:

1. According to the authors, why are children more heavily exposed to secondhand smoke than any other age group?
2. In the authors' view, what are the two main reasons why deaths resulting from secondhand smoke exposure are higher among women than men?
3. What two areas do the authors of the piece advise policy makers to implement with regard to educating the public about the hazards of secondhand smoke?

The harmful effects of second-hand smoke have been recorded since 1928. In the 1970s, scientific interest in potential adverse health effects of second-hand smoke expanded. Since then, evidence about ill health because of second-hand smoke has accumulated from many studies done in different parts of the world. However, second-hand smoke remains a common indoor air pollutant in many regions. Comprehensive legislation to protect non-smokers from exposure to second-hand smoke in all indoor workplaces and public places has been implemented in some countries and subnational jurisdictions, but 93% of the world's population is still living in countries not covered by fully smoke-free public health regulations. . . .

The Dangers of Secondhand Smoke

Exposure to second-hand smoke is still one of the most common indoor pollutants worldwide. On the basis of the proportions of second-hand smoke exposure, as many as 40% of children, 35% of women, and 33% of men are regularly exposed to second-hand smoke indoors. We noted wide regional variations of exposure, ranging from 13% or less in Africa to 50% or more in the western Pacific or eastern Europe. These differences can be mostly explained by the stages of the tobacco epidemic of a country because second-hand smoke is closely related to active smoking rates where no robust and extensive smoke-free indoor policies exist.

We have estimated that second-hand smoke caused 603,000 deaths and 10.9 million DALYs [disability-adjusted life years] worldwide in 2004, corresponding to 1.0% of all deaths and 0.7% of the worldwide burden of disease in DALYs in this year. These deaths should be added to the estimated 5.1 million deaths attributable to active smoking to obtain the full effect of both passive and active smoking. Smoking, therefore, was responsible for more than 5.7 million deaths every year in 2004. Worldwide, children are more heavily exposed to second-hand smoke than any other age-group, and they are not able to avoid the main source of exposure—mainly their close relatives who smoke at home. Furthermore, children are the group that has the strongest evidence of harm attributable to second-hand smoke. These two factors should form the basis of public health messages and advice to policy makers.

Almost two-thirds of all deaths in children and adults and a quarter of DALYs attributable to exposure to second-hand smoke were caused by ischaemic heart disease in adult non-smokers. Smoke-free laws banning smoking in indoor workplaces rapidly reduce numbers of acute coronary events. Therefore, policy makers should bear in mind that enforcing complete smoke-free laws will probably substantially reduce the number of deaths attributable to exposure to second-hand smoke within the first year of its implementation, with accompanying reduction in costs of illness in social and health systems.

Victims of Secondhand Smoke

The largest effects on deaths occurred in women. The absolute number of deaths is higher in women than in men for two main reasons. First, the number of female non-smokers (thus susceptible to be exposed to second-hand smoke by definition) is about 60% higher than that of male non-smokers. Second, in Africa and some parts of the Americas, the eastern Mediterranean, and southeast Asia, women are at least 50% more likely to be exposed to second-hand smoke than are men. Our data do not specify where the burden occurs; however, some setting-specific information about exposure is available. In the European Union, for example, exposure is almost equally distributed between the workplace and home, and women constitute about 40% of the workforce. In the western Pacific and east Asia, women equally constitute an important part of the workforce and about half of the women are exposed to second-hand smoke. In the eastern Mediterranean region, 32% of women, substantially more than the 22% of men, are exposed to second-hand smoke. Because these women constitute only 25% of the labour force, much of the exposure probably occurs at home.

We estimated that 165,000 children younger than 5 years die every year from lower respiratory infections caused by exposure to second-hand smoke. Two-thirds of these deaths occur in Africa and south Asia. Children's exposure to second-hand smoke most likely happens at home. The combination of infectious diseases and tobacco seems to be a deadly combination for children in these regions and might hamper the efforts to reduce the mortality rate for those aged younger than 5 years as sought by Millennium Development Goal 4. In addition to ischaemic heart disease in adults and asthma in children and adults, lower respiratory infections were also the cause of many DALYs lost because of second-hand smoke exposure. The largest burden of DALYs from second-hand smoke exposure was in children.

Information about the magnitude and distribution of the burden of disease caused by second-hand smoke is particularly pertinent to policy makers because the harm done by second-hand smoke is eminently preventable. There are well documented and effective interventions to reduce exposure to second-hand smoke in public and private places. For example, by the end of 2007, 16 countries had passed national smoke-free legislation covering all workplaces and public sites, and many other countries have state or local government ordinances that restrict smoking. In

"Oh no, secondhand smoke!!," cartoon by McCoy, Glenn and Gary, www.CartoonStock .com. Copyright © McCoy, Glenn and Gary. Reproduction rights obtainable from www .CartoonStock.com.

a review of the effectiveness of legislation of this type, exposure to second-hand smoke in high-risk settings (such as bars and restaurants) was typically reduced by about 90%, and the exposure of adult non-smokers in the general population to secondhand smoke cut by as much as 60%.

Alleviating the Burden

Most epidemiological studies have been done in developed countries. Conditions in developing countries can differ from those in high-income countries, and, in particular, exposure to second-hand smoke in the home is often not well characterized by the presence or absence of parents or spouses who smoke. Factors contributing to the differences in intensity of indoor exposure to second-hand smoke between developing and developed countries include: intensity of tobacco smoking (mean cigarettes and other smoking tobacco per day per smoker); natural ventilation (e.g., the climate allows open architectural structures or opening of windows); crowding at home (e.g., sharing of bedrooms with people who smoke); the pathogens most frequently associated with respiratory illnesses; smoke from solid fuels used for cooking; and enforcement of legal protection from exposure to second-hand smoke in indoor workplaces and public places. However, on the basis of the biomarker and epidemiological data reviewed and additional analyses done, we concluded that exposures in households in which someone smokes are broadly the same across regions, with higher intensities in Asia and the Middle East than in Europe, and lower levels in Latin America. Factors such as crowding, ventilation, and smoke from solid fuels seem to have little effect on actual exposure and health effects across regions on the basis of available evidence. . . .

Previously reported national estimates of the burden of disease caused by second-hand smoke are generally similar to those reported here. Variations result from differences in the burden from active smoking, the active and passive smoking rates used, and the methods used (e.g., whether or not active smokers are deemed susceptible). The size of the relative risk estimates used did not generally vary across studies of health effects from exposure to second-hand smoke.

This assessment shows that second-hand smoke poses a substantial health risk and disease burden for children and adult non-smokers worldwide. The findings are relevant to health policy decisions and public health strategies in all regions.

Only 7.4% of the world population lives in jurisdictions with comprehensive smoke-free laws at present, and the enforcement of these laws is robust in only a few of those jurisdictions. We recommend that the provisions of the WHO [World Health Organization] Framework Convention on Tobacco Control should be enforced immediately to create complete smoke-free environments in all indoor workplaces, public places, and on public transport. When policy makers implement these measures they are likely to record a substantial and rapid decline in the mortality attributable to tobacco and long-term reduction of DALYs lost from second-hand smoke. Fully smoke-free policies have a net positive effect on businesses, including the hospitality sector, and enforcement and education about smoke-free policies will have minimum costs to governments. Additionally, they are supported by much of the population, and this support increases after its enforcement—even in most smokers. In addition to the protection they offer to non-smokers, such smoke-free policies reduce cigarette consumption among continuing smokers and lead to increased successful cessation in smokers. Above all, these policies contribute decisively to denormalize smoking, and help with the approval and implementation of other policies that reduce tobacco demand, such as increased tobacco taxes and a comprehensive ban of tobacco advertising, promotion, and sponsorship.

Policy makers should also take action in two other areas to protect children and adults. First, although the benefits of smoke-free laws clearly extend to homes, protection of children and women from second-hand smoke in many regions needs to include complementary educational strategies to reduce exposure to second-hand smoke at home. Voluntary smoke-free home policies reduce exposure of children and adult non-smokers to second-hand smoke, reduce smoking in adults, and seem to reduce smoking in youths. Second, exposure to secondhand smoke contributes to the death of thousands of children younger than 5 years in low-income countries. Prompt attention is needed to dispel the myth that developing countries can wait to deal with tobacco-related diseases until they have dealt with infectious diseases. Together, tobacco smoke and infections lead to substantial, avoidable mortality and loss of active life-years of children.

| "If ANR were to inform an active smoker that his risk of heart disease was no different than that of a passive smoker, it would essentially represent malpractice." |

The Dangers of Secondhand Smoke Are Overblown

Michael Siegel

Michael Siegel is a professor in the Department of Community Health Sciences at the Boston University School of Public Health and has published nearly seventy papers on tobacco control. In the following viewpoint, Siegel argues that antismoking groups tend to inflate their data about the dangers of secondhand smoke, sometimes to the point of deception. He cites a study by the Americans for Nonsmokers' Rights (ANR) that concluded "there are virtually no health disparities between active and passive smoking." While Siegel concedes that secondhand smoke is not without health consequences, he believes such statements mislead the public about the actual health risks and hamper the credibility of all future research conducted on the topic.

As you read, consider the following questions:

1. What evidence does the author provide to support his case that the effects of secondhand smoke and active smoke are not the same with respect to heart disease?
2. In the author's view, what are two reasons he considers it "very misleading" to suggest "there are no health disparities" between active and passive smokers?
3. What inconsistency does the author claim is "interesting to note" with ANR's findings on the Whincup study?

A leading national advocacy group which promotes smoke-free policies and educates the public about the health effects of secondhand smoke is claiming that there are virtually no differences in health effects between active and passive smoking. Americans for Nonsmokers' Rights (ANR) makes the claim on its online fact sheet entitled: "Secondhand Smoke: The Science."

Specifically, ANR claims that: "there are virtually no health disparities between active and passive smoking."

ANR further claims that: "The risks of heart disease associated with secondhand smoke are twice what were previously thought and are virtually indistinguishable from those associated with active smoking."

ANR supports both claims by citing a single article written by Whincup PH, titled "Passive Smoking and Risk of Coronary Heart Disease and Stroke: Prospective Study with Cotinine Measurement."

Scientific Evidence Does Not Support ANR's Claim

ANR's claim that there are virtually no health disparities between active and passive smoking is unfortunately (or fortunately, depending on how you look at it) a lie.

I say fortunately because if ANR were being truthful in claiming that passive smoking has virtually the same level of

"In the olden days—smoking compared to leprosy," cartoon by Terry Wise, www.Cartoon Stock.com. Copyright © Terry Wise. Reproduction rights obtainable from www.Cartoon Stock.com. © Cartoonstock.com.

health effects as active smoking, then there would be tens of thousands more deaths from secondhand smoke than we currently observe.

I honestly don't understand how ANR can claim that there are virtually no health disparities between active and passive smoking. That implies that active smoking is virtually no more dangerous than exposure to secondhand smoke. We know this is not true, because there is a dose-response relationship between tobacco smoke exposure and lung cancer. The relative risk of lung cancer among active smokers is about 17, while the relative risk of lung cancer among passive smokers is about 1.3. How ANR can claim that 17 is "virtually" the same as 1.3 is beyond my understanding of basic mathematics.

Even if we restrict ourselves to the risk of heart disease, the scientific evidence simply doesn't support the conclusion that the risk of heart disease is "virtually" the same for active and passive smokers.

ANR acknowledges that the relative risk for heart disease associated with passive smoking is about 1.5 or 1.6. A very large and perhaps the most recent study of the relative risk of heart disease among active smokers (the Nurses Health Study) revealed a relative risk of 3.12 for women smoking 1-14 cigarettes per day and 5.48 for women smoking 15 or more cigarettes per day. The CDC [Centers for Disease Control and Prevention] estimates that the overall relative risk for heart disease mortality associated with secondhand smoke exposure is about 2.0 (this is going to be lower than the relative risk associated with the incidence of heart disease). There are a few studies which suggest that the long-term relative risk for heart disease may be on the order of about 1.3 for light active smokers of just 1–9 cigarettes per day (this is what Whincup et al. found). Thus, even if we restrict ourselves to the risk for heart disease, it is not accurate to state that the effects of secondhand smoke and active smoking are virtually the same. There appears to be a clear dose-response relationship (albeit a non-linear one, unlike for lung cancer), and for active smokers of a half pack per day or more, the risk of heart disease is undeniably substantially higher than for passive smokers.

The Whincup study itself does not support ANR's contention that there are virtually no health disparities between active and passive smoking. The article makes no such claim.

Moreover, the Whincup article does not even claim that there are no health disparities between active and passive smoking with regards to heart disease. While the article does find that for very light active smokers (less than half pack per day), the short-term relative risks for heart disease are similar to those among passive smokers, it is very misleading to represent this finding as establishing that there are no health disparities in the risk of heart disease between active and passive smokers. First, the risk of heart disease among the majority of active smokers (who smoke half pack per day or more) is substantially higher than among passive smokers. Second, . . . even among light active smokers, upon long-term follow-up there is a clear divergence in the heart disease risk compared to passive smokers.

Flawed Findings

If ANR were to inform an active smoker that his risk of heart disease was no different than that of a passive smoker, it would essentially represent malpractice, because unless this smoker is an extremely light smoker, the information is undeniably false. Such advice could encourage a smoker to continue smoking rather than to quit, because it minimizes the true health effects of active smoking.

It is also interesting to note that while ANR is apparently so impressed by the importance of the Whincup study, it fails to inform the public that the very same study found no significant increase in stroke risk among passive smokers. Yet ANR claims in its fact sheet that: "There is a link between secondhand smoke to an increased risk of stroke." Here, ANR cites a different study.

It appears that ANR is just cherry-picking the studies it wants to in order to support the claims that it wants to make. If the Whincup study is so reliable that it can be counted on in making the claim that passive smoking causes heart disease, then why is the very same study unreliable when it finds that passive smoking in the very same subjects did not increase their risk of stroke?

By the way, I am not arguing here that secondhand smoke is not related to stroke risk. I believe that if one looks at the overall evidence, there does appear to be a causal link. However, I am just pointing out that ANR's approach of simply citing a specific study here or there to support its claims is tantamount to cherry-picking, especially when they ignore findings from the very studies they are citing.

The rest of the story is that ANR's "fact sheet" which is purportedly bringing us "The Science" on secondhand smoke is actually telling us a lie when it claims that "there are virtually no health disparities between active and passive smoking." There are, in fact, very important dose-related health disparities, and it is critical that the public appreciate the dose-response nature of the relationship between tobacco smoke exposure and adverse health effects.

I do not believe it is necessary for ANR to lie like this in order to impress upon the public the damaging health effects associated with secondhand smoke. I think the truth is certainly enough.

Periodical and Internet
Sources Bibliography

The following articles have been selected to supplement the diverse views presented in this chapter.

American Legacy Foundation	"Impact of Tobacco on the Environment," April 2010, www .legacyforhealth.org.
John Banzhaf	"Smoker's Breath Creates Indoor Air Pollution 'Harmful' to Children and Perhaps Adults," *Action on Smoking and Health (ASH)*, June 22, 2008.
Jonathan Benson	"Smoking Habits Passed from Father to Son, Mother to Daughter, Study Finds," *Natural News*, February 19, 2011.
John Reid Blackwell	"Altria: Smoking Is Addictive," *Richmond Times-Dispatch,* May 19, 2011.
Jose L. Castillo	"Panel Talks Tobacco Control," *Harvard Crimson*, April 13, 2011.
The Economist	"Out of Puff: Where Smoking Kills Most People," October 29, 2009.
Jay Fitzgerald	"Ban on Hiring Smokers Blasted," *Boston Herald,* November 27, 2010.
Gardiner Harris	"Review Casts More Doubts on a Lung Cancer Study," *New York Times*, April 29, 2011.
US Department of Health and Human Services	"How Tobacco Smoke Causes Disease: The Biology and Behavioral Basis for Smoking-Attributable Disease," *American Banker*, vol. 170, no. 121, June 24, 2005, p. 11.
Roger Watson, David Fritz, Cindy Corell, and Jim McCloskey	"Images or Not, Tobacco Isn't Pretty," *Staunton News Leader*, June 23, 2011.

Should Tobacco Use Be Regulated?

Chapter Preface

In June 2006, attorney John Birke filed a lawsuit against the owners of the Oakwood Apartments in Woodland Hills, California, claiming that they were liable for secondhand smoke that compromised the health of his five-year-old asthma-stricken daughter, Melinda. Birke's complaint, which sought unspecified general and special damages, alleged that in allowing tenants and visitors to smoke in outdoor common areas on the premises, Oakwood's management was guilty of creating a public nuisance. Birke's attorney, Michael R. Sohigian, stated in court documents that as landlords, the complex's ownership had a basic duty to protect tenants from exposure to "unreasonable risk of harm." Though the case was thrown out in 2007, a state appellate court reinstated Birke's suit in a subsequent unanimous three-justice ruling and on January 13, 2009, Sohigian declared he and his client to be "gratified . . . that a California court [was] the first in the nation to hold [that] secondhand smoke is a public nuisance."

Laws creating nonsmoking sections in airplanes and restaurants have existed since Minnesota enacted its statewide Clean Indoor Air Act in 1975. A decade later, Aspen, Colorado, was the first city in the United States to ban smoking in restaurants. Increasingly sterner and controversial measures have followed, from San Luis Obispo, California's 1990 ban on indoor smoking at any public place to entire cities being declared smoke-free everywhere but in residential homes. As of April 2011, thirty-seven states had some form of a smoking ban.

Advocates of smoking bans assert that the rationale for smoking bans is elemental: Smoking is optional and breathing is not. The smokers are therefore infringing on the breathing rights of the nonsmokers. Evidence compiled by the American Cancer Society cites that cigarette smoke contains more than 250 toxins and carcinogens; the risks of getting lung cancer rise by 30 percent for nonsmokers inhaling secondhand or sidestream smoke (which refers to smoke dispersed in the air rather than being directly inhaled). Other potential hazards of smoke inhalation range from brain tumors and heart disease to lung, breast or cervical cancer, which can then metastasize throughout the body.

Yet, compared to other forms of industrialized air pollution, secondhand smoke barely registers as a blip. According to the World Health Organization, 2.4 million people die every year as the result of air pollution, more than half of them attributable to fine particles spewed as the result of power plant emissions or engine exhaust. And while air pollution from automobiles kills more people per year than car accidents, there is little organized outcry for a worldwide ban on motor vehicles. At what point do restrictions on personal liberty become unreasonable? And is tobacco unfairly singled out as an easy target?

The following viewpoints in this chapter explore the various sides of the debate over government's role in legislating tobacco use and the morality of collecting taxes and lawsuit settlements from the manufacturers of products sold and advertised to the general public.

> *"Every ban on smoking . . . sends a very clear educational message to the smoker that his conduct is not desirable."*

Smoking Bans in Public Places Are Beneficial

Action on Smoking and Health (ASH)

Action on Smoking and Health (ASH) is a national nonprofit legal action and educational organization that lobbies for stricter non-smoking legislation and fights for the legal rights of nonsmokers. In the following viewpoint, the author argues that there are numerous reasons for imposing smoking bans in public places. The author claims that in addition to the obvious health hazards caused or inflamed by secondhand smoke, ordinances prohibiting smoking in public areas also cut down on littering, improve the health of local wildlife, and send positive messages to children and smokers trying to quit by reinforcing the idea that smoking is socially unacceptable and carries with it a powerful stigma.

As you read, consider the following questions:

1. According to the viewpoint's author, what "rights" does society recognize people have with regard to carcinogens,

and what are examples the author cites in which such substances are taken seriously by legislators?

2. In the author's view, what are two benefits of public smoking bans that are unrelated to inhaling smoke?

3. In what ways cited by the author does public smoking impact the environment?

Reasons for Banning Smoking in Certain Public Outdoor Areas

1. Careful scientific studies—based upon both highly accurate mathematical modeling techniques as well as actual real-life measurements—have shown that concentrations of secondhand tobacco smoke in many outdoor areas are often as high or higher than in some indoor areas and that the risks posed by such outdoor exposure, while small to most individuals, are well beyond generally accepted norms when large numbers of people are involuntarily exposed. Indeed, for these very reasons, the State of California—in a report summarizing much of this evidence—was preparing and has now declared OUTDOOR tobacco smoke as a "toxic air pollutant."

2. Drifting tobacco smoke, even outdoors, can trigger asthmatic attacks, bronchial infections, and other serious health problems in non-smokers. This is especially true for the almost 100 million Americans who have asthma, chronic bronchitis, chronic sinusitis, emphysema, and other breathing-related conditions which make them especially susceptible to secondhand tobacco smoke.

3. Even for people without such respiratory conditions, breathing drifting tobacco smoke for even brief periods can be deadly. For example, the Centers for Disease Control [CDC] has warned that breathing drifting tobacco smoke for as little as 30 minutes (less than the time one might be exposed outdoors on a beach, sitting on a

park bench, listening to a concert in a park, etc.) can raise a non-smoker's risk of suffering a fatal heart attack to that of a smoker. The danger is even greater for those who are already at an elevated risk for coronary problems: e.g., men over 40 and postmenopausal women, anyone who is obese, has diabetes, a personal or family history of heart or circulatory conditions, gets insufficient exercise, has high blood pressure, cholesterol, etc.

4. In cases where drifting tobacco smoke was present and a non-smoker suffered a heart attack, asthmatic attack, or other similar problems, the municipality [that] owns and operates the beach, park, playground, etc. could be liable since it was on notice of the known health dangers but failed to take the "reasonable" step of banning smoking as taken by many other outdoor areas.

5. Society recognizes that people have a right not to be involuntarily exposed to known carcinogenic substances, even if only to small amounts and for brief periods. That's why, for example, extensive and very expensive precautions are taken when asbestos is removed from buildings. This ensures that people outside are not exposed even to minute amounts as they pass by. Similarly, we would not tolerate someone who filed down old brake drums in a playground, thereby releasing even tiny amounts of asbestos into the air. Secondhand tobacco smoke is officially classified by the federal government as a "known human carcinogen"—exactly the same category as asbestos.

6. Even aside from health hazards, being forced to breathe tobacco smoke is annoying and irritating to most people, especially the almost 100 million Americans who have chronic conditions like asthma and bronchitis which make them especially susceptible to tobacco smoke, and young children who are also especially sensitive. It should be noted that many activities are banned in public places

Public Smoking Bans Are Good for the Heart

Secondhand smoke exposure [is harmful to the heart in many ways; it] alters platelet function, causes endothelial dysfunction, increases arterial stiffness, decreases levels of high-density lipoprotein, increases markers of inflammation, increases arterial intima-media thickening, increases infarct size, causes oxidative stress and mitochondrial damage, decreases heart rate variability (thus increasing the risk of malignant arrhythmias), and increases insulin resistance. It is hard to imagine substances that would be more cardiotoxic. Furthermore, these adverse effects are observed at very low exposure doses.

Steven A. Schroeder, "Public Smoking Bans Are Good for the Heart," Journal of the American College of Cardiology, *vol. 54, no. 14, 2009, pp. 1256–1257.*

simply because they are annoying or irritating, even if they do not pose a health hazard. Common examples are playing loud music on portable radios or boom boxes, engaging in sexually provocative activity, using profanity, dressing in inappropriately scanty attire, drinking alcoholic beverages, etc.

7. Many of the 96 million Americans who have chronic conditions like asthma and bronchitis which make them especially susceptible to tobacco smoke have been held to be entitled to protection under the Americans with Disabilities Act [ADA]. Thus, if their medical conditions mean that they cannot enjoy lying on a blanket at the

beach or in a park for a concert where smoking is generally permitted, they may be entitled by law to a reasonable accommodation, presumably one [that] protects them from drifting tobacco smoke.

8. The reason for banning smoke around building entrances is simple. People should not be forced to be exposed to known carcinogenic substances for even the briefest periods of time, and because even brief exposure can also be annoying and irritating to many people, non-smokers should not be forced to "run a gauntlet" of smokers gathered around the exits and entrances to their workplaces, or other buildings which they are likely to frequent.

9. Large buildings ordinarily have air intakes to replace the air which is exhausted by their ventilation systems. Occasionally, the air intake will be located near a doorway to the building, or in some other area where smokers might tend to congregate. Therefore, to prevent this smoke-filled air from entering and being circulated throughout the building where it can create a health risk as well as annoyance and physical irritation, it may be necessary to prohibit smoking outdoors around such air intakes.

10. Cigarette butts discarded by smokers constitute the overwhelming majority of litter on beaches, as well as in many other public places like parks, playgrounds, and sidewalks. Smoking bans have been shown to substantially reduce the litter and therefore the costs of cleaning up beaches and other outdoor areas, as well as to improve the overall appearance and attractiveness of the area.

11. Cigarettes are a major source of burns to youngsters, including to their faces, when smokers hold their cigarettes at their sides and young children inadvertently come too close. This can happen easily when children are at play or otherwise distracted on a beach, waiting on a line while

their parents wait to buy tickets, to use an ATM machine, etc.—and once again there may be legal liability.

12. Discarded cigarettes—which are designed to continue to burn for several minutes when dropped and not puffed upon—are also a major fire hazard, threatening piers, boardwalks, and wooden structures in parks and playgrounds, etc., as well as outdoor park and recreation areas.

13. Young children playing in the sand at a beach or in [a] playground sandbox may be tempted to put cigarette butts—which contain concentrated amounts of carcinogens and other toxic chemicals trapped from tobacco smoke—into their mouths, and even older children may touch the cigarette butts and then put their fingers in or near their mouths, eyes, etc.

14. Discarded cigarette butts may also be harmful to birds and other wildlife which nibble on or even swallow them, especially on a beach or park, but also even on a public sidewalk. Indeed, one of the first domestic bans on outdoor smoking was enacted to protect wildlife rather than human beings.

15. Activities and images which might be inappropriate for young children and/or which might lead them into bad habits are often prohibited in public places, even if they pose no health risk and might even be appropriate in areas visited voluntarily only by adults. For example, virtually all municipalities have long prohibited consumption of alcoholic beverages in public places like parks and beaches. The purpose is obviously not to prevent drunkenness or driving while intoxicated—since people can easily get drunk drinking in their parked cars, in bars, and at home. Rather, bans are imposed because drinking sets a bad example for young children to see it done openly—even if the same children might see it in their own homes. Similarly, prohibiting smoking in

outdoor places frequented by the public—like parks, playgrounds, beaches, etc.—shields young children from seeing smoking as a common adult behavior to be emulated, even if some may observe smoking by the parents and other adults in private homes. Other examples where activities are prohibited in public places because of their possible impact on children include sexually suggestive movements (permitted on dance floors but prohibited in parks and on sidewalks), gambling (permitted in casinos and tracks but not in public places), displays of pictorial nudity (permitted in art galleries but not on sidewalks), etc.

16. In addition to all of the above reasons, it has now become clear that restrictions on smoking are a major factor in helping to persuade smokers to quit, and to help those who want to stop smoking to do so. The result can be an enormous saving of lives, in the prevention of disability, and in a dramatic reduction in health care costs—most of which are borne by non-smokers who otherwise are forced to pay higher taxes and inflated health insurance premiums. Smoking bans—including outdoors as well as indoors—encourage and support quitting by making it more inconvenient for a person to remain a smoker. Every ban on smoking also sends a very clear educational message to the smoker that his conduct is not desirable— and indeed is found to be annoying and irritating if not repugnant—by a large majority of others. Finally, smoking bans help those already trying to quit by tending to assure that they will not be tempted by being in the presence of a smoker, smell the "tempting" aroma of tobacco smoke, etc. While not the primary argument or purpose in enacting outdoor smoking bans, this additional significant effect of such bans may well be a factor in deciding to support such public health measures.

Support Increases for Outdoor Smoking Bans

More than 350 jurisdictions have successfully prohibited smoking in outdoor areas—such as beaches, parks, playgrounds, near building entrances, while waiting in lines, etc.—without legal challenges, problems of enforcement, loss of patronage or taxes, etc. Such bans appear to be so successful that more jurisdictions are sure to be added. Indeed, as smoking is being banned in an ever growing number of indoor areas, people are beginning to expect freedom from these toxic fumes, and to expect air unpolluted by tobacco smoke wherever they may congregate.

Very strong recent evidence of this trend is the overwhelming vote by the citizens of the State of Washington to ban smoking not only in all bars and restaurant[s], but to also require that building entrances be smokefree, and to prohibit smoking within 25 feet of doorways, windows, and ventilation ducts of smokefree establishments. This vote comes on the heels of a poll by the New York State Health Department which showed that the public support for banning smoking in many outdoor areas is even stronger than similar support for a 2003 bill banning indoor smoking.

"Smoking bans reduce public welfare by preventing an optimal allocation of non-smoking and smoking-permitted public places."

Smoking Bans Are Ineffective

Thomas A. Lambert

Thomas A. Lambert is an associate professor at the University of Missouri-Columbia School of Law. In the following piece, Lambert maintains that public smoking bans are not only ineffective, but in some ways are even more harmful to the public than secondhand smoke itself. He argues that not only are nonsmokers "compensated" for suffering inconveniences and risks virtually anywhere outside their homes, but the amount of carcinogens they inhaled from secondhand smoke pales in comparison to those which they are regularly exposed to from other forms of pollution that are exempt from federal or state bans. Moreover, demonizing cigarette smoking only serves to make it "cooler" in the eyes of the impressionable youths such bans are allegedly protecting, he says. In addition, the widely held assertion that the health costs of caring for smokers who have contracted heart disease, lung cancer, or other ailments as a result of their smoking are disproportionately borne by the general public is, in Lambert's view, a myth, because smokers provide savings in medical expenses by dying sooner than nonsmokers.

As you read, consider the following questions:

1. According to the author, how are nonsmokers "compensated" for tolerating indoor air pollution at certain facilities and how is this separate from a patron's outdoor air rights?
2. In the author's view, how do sweeping smoking bans make smoking more popular?
3. How does the author claim that smoking bans are not analogous to mandatory seat belt laws?

In recent months, dozens of localities and a number of states have enacted sweeping smoking bans. The bans generally forbid smoking in "public" places, which are defined to include not only publicly owned facilities but also privately owned properties to which members of the public are invited (e.g., bars, restaurants, hotel lobbies, etc.). Proponents of the bans insist that they are necessary to reduce risks to public health and welfare and to protect the rights of non-smoking patrons and employees of the regulated establishments.

Specifically, ban advocates have offered three justifications for government-imposed bans: First, they claim that such bans are warranted because indoor smoking involves a "negative externality," the market failure normally invoked to justify regulation of the ambient environment. In addition, advocates assert that smoking bans shape individual preferences against smoking, thereby reducing the number of smokers in society. Finally, proponents argue that smoking bans are justified, regardless of whether any market failure is present, simply because of the health risks associated with inhalation of environmental tobacco smoke (ETS), commonly referred to as "secondhand smoke."

This [viewpoint] contends that government-imposed smoking bans cannot be justified as responses to market failure, as means of shaping preferences, or on risk-reduction grounds. Smoking bans reduce public welfare by preventing an optimal allocation of non-smoking and smoking-permitted public places. A laissez-faire approach better accommodates heterogeneous preferences regarding public smoking.

The Externality Argument

The conventional justification for regulation of the ambient environment (i.e., outdoor air and water) is that it is necessary to combat the inefficiencies created by negative externalities. Negative externalities are costs that are not borne by the party in charge of the process that creates them. For example, the owner of a smoke-spewing factory does not fully bear the costs associated with the smoke, stench, and health risks his factory produces; many of those costs are foisted onto the factory's neighbors. When conduct involves negative externalities, participants will tend to engage in that conduct to an excessive degree, for they bear the full benefits, but not the full costs, of their activities. Quite often, then, government intervention (e.g., taxing the cost-creating behavior or limiting the amount permitted) may be desirable as a means of ensuring that the cost-creator does not engage to an excessive degree in the conduct at issue.

Advocates of smoking bans insist that indoor smoking involves negative externalities. First, ban advocates argue that non-smoking patrons and employees of establishments that allow smoking are forced to bear costs over which they have no control. In addition, smokers impose negative externalities in the form of increased health care costs, a portion of which is paid from the public fisc. Thus, taxpayers are required to foot the bill for some of the costs associated with smoking in general. Examined closely, each of these externality-based arguments for smoking bans fails.

Patrons and Employees

Outdoor air pollution involves the sort of negative externality likely to result in both an inoptimal (i.e., excessive) amount of the polluting activity and a violation of pollution victims' rights.

When it comes to indoor air pollution, by contrast, there is no such externality. That is because the individual charged with determining how much, if any, smoking is permitted in an indoor space ultimately bears the full costs of his or her decision and is thus likely to select the optimal level of air cleanliness. Moreover, non-smokers' "rights" are not violated, because they are compensated for the inconveniences and risks they suffer.

One might wonder how this could be. Because smokers in a public space impose costs on non-smoking patrons, who cannot order the smokers to stop, will indoor smoking not entail both the inefficiency (an excessive level of pollution) and the injustice (an infringement of non-polluters' rights to enjoy clean air) associated with outdoor air pollution? In a word, no. There is a crucial difference between outdoor and indoor air, and that difference alleviates the inefficiencies and rights-violations normally associated with air pollution.

The crucial difference is property rights. Whereas outdoor air is common property (and thus subject to the famous Tragedy of the Commons), the air inside a building is, in essence, "owned" by the building owner. That means that the building owner, who is in a position to control the amount of smoking (if any) that is permitted in the building, has an incentive to permit the "right" amount of smoking—that is, the amount that maximizes the welfare of individuals within the building. Depending on the highest and best use of the space and the types of people who patronize the building, the optimal level of smoking may be zero (as in an art museum), or "as much as patrons desire" (as in a tobacco lounge), or something in-between (as in most restaurants, which have smoking and non-smoking sections). Because patrons select establishments based on the benefits and costs of patronage, they will avoid establishments with air policies they do not like or will, at a minimum, reduce the amount they are willing to pay for goods and services at such places. Owners of public places thus bear the full costs and benefits of their decisions regarding air quality and can be expected to select the optimal level of air cleanliness. Moreover, customers who do not like the air policy a space-owner has selected will patronize the space only if they are being otherwise compensated by some positive attribute of the space at issue—say, cheap drinks or a particularly attractive clientele. They are, in other words, compensated for any "rights" violation. The de facto property rights that exist in indoor air, then, prevent the inefficiencies and injustices that accompany outdoor air pollution.

But what about workers at businesses that permit smoking? Is there not an externality in that they are forced to bear costs (and assume risks) over which they have no control? Again, the answer is no. Workers exercise control by demanding higher pay to compensate them for the risks and unpleasantries they experience because of the smoke in their workplaces. Adam Smith theorized about such "risk premiums" when he wrote in *The Wealth of Nations*:

> The whole of the advantages and disadvantages of the different employments of labor and stock must, in the same neighborhood, be either perfectly equal or tending to equality. . . . [T]he wages of labor vary with the ease or hardship, the honorableness or dishonorableness of employment.

He was right. A vast body of empirical evidence, including most notably that produced by economist W. Kip Viscusi, demonstrates that employers do in fact pay a premium for exposing their workers to risks and unpleasantries. Such risk/unpleasantry premiums motivate employers to select the optimal amount of smoke in their restaurants. They also alleviate any injustices occasioned by what might otherwise appear to be a violation of employees' rights. Thus, smoking in public establishments does not, in any meaningful sense, impose genuine negative externalities in the form of risks and unpleasantries to the patrons and employees of such establishments. Any externalities produced are merely "pecuniary" externalities—that is, externalities that are mitigated by the price mechanism and thus do not create inefficiencies and injustices.

Public Costs

Ban advocates also seek to justify prohibitions by pointing to externalities in the form of public health care expenditures. The argument here proceeds as follows:

- Smokers face disproportionately high health care costs.
- A portion of such costs is borne not by smokers themselves but by the public at large.
- Smokers thereby externalize some of the costs of their behavior and thus will tend to engage in "too much" smoking.
- Therefore, smoking bans are justified as an effort to cut back on the level of smoking that would otherwise exist.

This argument suffers from several weaknesses. First and most importantly, the initial premise is unsound. According to a comprehensive study in the *New England Journal of Medicine* in 1997, smoking probably has the effect of reducing overall health care costs because smokers die earlier than non-smokers. The study's authors concluded that in a population in which no one smoked, health care costs would be 7 percent higher among men and 4 percent higher among women than the costs in the current mixed population of smokers and non-smokers. The authors further determined that if all smokers were to quit, health care costs would be lower at first, but after 15 years they would become higher than at present.

Even if smoking were shown to increase public health care expenditures, the argument here would seem to prove too much. If increased health care costs could justify government imposition of a smoking ban in privately owned places, could they not similarly justify governmental regulation of menus at fast food restaurants or mandatory exercise regimens? Serious liberty interests would be at stake if a government were to make its citizens "be healthy" so as not to impose health care costs on others.

Finally, the assumption that public smoking bans reduce the incidence of smoking seems suspect. As discussed below, widespread smoking bans may actually increase the incidence of smoking among young people. Externalities in the form of increased public health care costs, then, likely cannot justify widespread bans on smoking in public spaces.

The Preference-Shaping Argument

The argument above concludes that smoking bans are unnecessary because market processes will ensure either that patrons' and employees' preferences regarding smoking are honored or that those individuals are compensated for not receiving their preferences. That argument assumes, though, that individuals' preferences are unaffected by the legal rule itself. A number of scholars have disputed the notion of "exogenous preferences." Instead, they claim that individuals' preferences regarding activities like smoking are influenced by the background legal rules themselves. Some theorists have therefore sought to justify smoking bans on grounds that they make smokers less likely to want to smoke and/or make non-smokers more likely to appreciate smoke-free environments and thus more willing to pay a premium for such environments. In the end, neither preference-shaping argument can justify widespread bans on public smoking.

Shaping Attitudes

In recent years, legal scholars have produced a voluminous literature on the role of law in indirectly controlling conduct by shaping social norms and individual preferences. Smoking bans provide one of the favorite "success stories" of those who laud the use of legal rules to change norms and preferences. According to these scholars, smoking bans affect behavior, even if under-enforced, because they change the social norm regarding smoking in public. With the advent of smoking bans, non-smokers who previously felt embarrassed about publicly expressing their distaste for ETS are speaking up. By providing a de facto community statement that public smoking is unacceptable, the bans embolden non-smokers to confront smokers who are inconveniencing them. Facing heightened public hostility toward their habits, smokers are likely to revise their preferences regarding smoking. Thus, by making smoking more socially costly, the theory goes, bans reduce the number of smokers.

Of course, this is a good thing only if actual social utility is increased by reducing the incidence of smoking. Ban advocates assume that reducing smoking is welfare-enhancing for the obvious reason that smoking carries serious health risks. But ban advocates generally are not in a position to judge the cost side of reducing smoking because they do not know the degree of utility smokers experience by smoking. Smokers themselves, who these days are aware of the risks of smoking, appear to believe that the benefits they experience from the activity outweigh the costs. It is thus not at all clear that eliminating smoking will enhance social welfare.

But even if it were clear that society would be better off with less smoking, attempting to use smoking bans to influence social norms may not represent wise policy. Sweeping smoking bans may actually increase the incidence of smoking. A large percentage of smokers acquire the habit at a young age, and they frequently do so because smoking is "cool." Smoking is cool, of course, because it is rebellious. The harder anti-smoking forces work to coerce people into quitting smoking, and the more they engage the government and other establishment institutions in their efforts, the more rebellious—and thus the "cooler"—smoking becomes. Even advocates of the use of smoking regulation to alter social norms acknowledge that overly intrusive regulations may result in this sort of "norm backlash." As an empirical matter, then, it is not clear whether sweeping smoking bans—highly intrusive regulatory interventions—actually reduce the incidence of smoking in the long run. . . .

The Risk Argument

The first two arguments for smoking bans focus, to some degree, on citizens' preferences: the externality argument focuses on a purported market failure that allegedly prevents the satisfaction of preferences regarding smoking, and the preference-shaping argument focuses on the law's inevitable role in shaping those preferences. By contrast, the third common argument for smoking bans ignores citizens' smoking preferences altogether. That argument asserts that smoking should be banned in public places, regardless of individuals' smoking preferences, because the health risks it presents are simply too great. In other words, smoking bans are justified on risk-based grounds even if there is no need to remedy a market failure or to correct a preference-shaping bias in the law.

Policymakers frequently invoke excessive risk as a sufficient ground for regulating an activity, even when that activity does not involve a market failure or reflect preferences that have been skewed by the background legal rules. Consider, for example, mandatory seatbelt laws. There is not much of an externality involved in the failure to wear a seatbelt because the costs of the conduct are borne by the person deciding to engage in it. While mandatory seatbelt laws may have the effect of altering preferences, there is no reason to think that the background legal rule had previously biased preferences against wearing seatbelts, and risk-avoidance is the sole reason for altering citizen preferences in the first place. Thus, the predominant justification for mandatory seatbelt laws, which have been enacted in every state except "Live Free or Die" New Hampshire, is risk-reduction—not externalities or a need to shape preferences for some end other than risk-reduction. Similarly, ban advocates argue, public smoking bans may be justified solely on grounds of risk-avoidance.

Unreliable Findings

But a purely risk-based argument likely cannot justify a sweeping smoking ban. While risk, standing alone, is sometimes deemed sufficient to justify government prohibition of private conduct, such prohibition seems appropriate only when the harm avoided is relatively great and the regulation's intrusion on personal liberty is relatively small. Again, consider mandatory seatbelt laws. The risk associated with not wearing a seatbelt is huge, and the regulation's intrusion on personal liberty is minor—no more than a slight inconvenience. Hence, the laws may be justifiable on risk-reduction grounds. Consider, by comparison, whether the government could invoke risk as a legitimate basis for banning driving after 1:00 A.M. Such behavior certainly presents a heightened risk (late-night drivers are far more likely to fall asleep at the wheel), but the magnitude of risk presented does not justify the degree of liberty intrusion occasioned by the regulation. Smoking bans look more like late-night driving bans than mandatory seatbelt laws and thus likely cannot be justified solely with reference to risk.

To see why this is so, we must first isolate the relevant risk. Because public smoking bans do not prohibit smoking altogether and may not even reduce its incidence, the risk the bans aim to avert is not the risk to smokers themselves. It is instead the risk to non-smokers—i.e., the risks associated with inhalation of ETS. The key question, then, is whether these risks are of sufficient magnitude to justify a significant intrusion on the personal liberty of private business owners and their customers.

If one were to rely on the stated conclusions of federal agencies (and/or the media reports discussing those conclusions), one might conclude that the risks associated with ETS inhalation do justify significant liberty restrictions. First consider the Environmental Protection Agency [EPA]'s 1992 report, *Respiratory Health Effects of Passive Smoking: Lung Cancer and Other Disorders*. That study, which concluded that ETS is a Class A (known human) carcinogen, purported to show that inhalation

"Tobacconist: No Smoking," cartoon by Chris Madden. Copyright © Chris Madden. www .chrismadden.co.uk. Reproduced by permission.

of ETS causes 3,000 lung cancer deaths per year. Not surprisingly, the study fueled efforts to impose smoking bans.

As it turns out, the study hardly amounted to sound science. A congressional inquiry into the methods the EPA used in the study found that "the process at every turn [was] characterized by both scientific and procedural irregularities," including "conflicts

of interest by both Agency staff involved in the preparation of
the risk assessment and members of the Science Advisory Board
panel selected to provide a supposedly independent evaluation
of the document." The congressional inquiry further concluded
that "the Agency ha[d] deliberately abused and manipulated the
scientific data in order to reach a predetermined, politically motivated result."

The findings of the EPA's 1992 study have also been undermined by court opinion. Charged with evaluating the agency's risk
assessment in determining that ETS constitutes a Class A carcinogen, a federal district judge in the case *Flue-Cured Tobacco Coop.
Stabilization Corp. v. U.S. EPA* criticized the agency's analysis in
terms that can best be described as scathing. The court concluded:

> [The EPA] publicly committed to a conclusion before research
> had begun; . . . adjusted established procedure and scientific
> norms to validate the Agency's public conclusion[;] . . . disre-
> garded information and made findings on selective informa-
> tion; did not disseminate significant epidemiologic informa-
> tion; deviated from its Risk Assessment Guidelines; failed to
> disclose important findings and reasoning; and left significant
> questions without answers.

Thus, the EPA's purported finding that ETS poses a serious
cancer risk—a "finding" that has been extremely influential in
motivating state and local smoking bans throughout the United
States, should be discounted.

Apparently undeterred by these congressional and judicial
reprimands, the U.S. surgeon general recently released a report entitled *The Health Consequences of Involuntary Exposure
to Tobacco Smoke*, which purports to settle once and for all the
debate over the risks of ETS inhalation. In releasing the report,
Surgeon General Richard Carmona confidently proclaimed:

> The scientific evidence is now indisputable: secondhand
> smoke is not a mere annoyance. It is a serious health hazard

that can lead to disease and premature death in children and nonsmoking adults.

In presenting the report, the surgeon general's office emphasized to the news media that even brief exposure to ETS poses immediate and significant health risks. The press release accompanying the report stated that "there is no risk-free level of exposure to secondhand smoke" and that "even brief exposure to secondhand smoke has immediate adverse effects on the cardiovascular system and increases risk for heart disease and lung cancer." In his remarks to the media, the surgeon general stated, "Breathing secondhand smoke for even a short time can damage cells and set the cancer process in motion." In a "fact sheet" accompanying the report, the surgeon general explained, "Breathing secondhand smoke for even a short time can have immediate adverse effects on the cardiovascular system." These and similar statements, faithfully repeated by the news media, create the impression that science has determined that simply being in a smoke-filled room exposes one to significant health risks.

Examined closely, the surgeon general's report established no such proposition. The underlying studies upon which the surgeon general's report was based considered the effects of chronic exposure to ETS on individuals, such as long-time spouses of smokers. The studies simply did not consider the health effects of sporadic exposure to ETS and thus cannot provide empirical support for the surgeon general's statements about short-term ETS exposure.

Moreover, those statements are theoretically unsound, for they conflict with the basic toxicological principle that "the dose makes the poison." According to a study published in the *New England Journal of Medicine* in 1975, when many more individuals smoked and there were much higher ETS concentrations in public places, exposure to an hour's worth of prevailing levels of ETS was equivalent to smoking 0.004 cigarettes. Put differently, one would have to breathe smoke-filled air for 4,000 hours in order to inhale as much tobacco smoke as a smoker inhales in a single cigarette. Given those concentration levels, it seems implausible that short-term exposure to ETS poses serious health risks. Possessing neither empirical foundation nor theoretical plausibility, the Surgeon General's public statements about the health risks of brief exposure to ETS were misleading.

But what about the actual findings of the surgeon general's report, as opposed to the hyperbolic (and widely reported) accompanying statements? Those findings—even taken at face value—do not provide a risk-based rationale for highly intrusive smoking bans. The report concludes that chronic ETS exposure increases the risks of lung cancer and heart disease by 20 to 30 percent. While those numbers sound fairly large, one must remember that the underlying risks of lung cancer and heart disease in non-smokers are quite small to begin with. A 20 percent increase in a tiny risk is, well, really tiny—certainly too tiny to justify the substantial liberty infringement involved in smoking bans. Indeed, risk alone has not justified a ban on smoking itself, an activity that increases the risk of heart disease by 100 to 300 percent and that of lung cancer by 900 percent. How, then, could a much smaller risk justify highly intrusive regulation of the voluntary actions of individuals gathered on private property? . . .

The Superiority of Laissez-Faire

Controversies over smoking in public places are ultimately controversies over property rights. Does a smoker have the right to fill the air with his or her smoke, or do non-smokers have the right to smoke-free air? In other words, who "owns" the air? A smoking ban effectively gives nonsmoking patrons the right to the air. By contrast, the laissez-faire approach effectively permits the owner of the establishment to determine the proper allocation of air rights within his or her space. The owner may choose to give the rights to smoking patrons (by permitting smoking), non-smokers (by banning smoking), or to try to accommodate both by designating some parts of the establishment nonsmoking but permitting smoking elsewhere within the space.

However owners allocate the right to air among smokers and non-smokers, there will be some "winners" whose preferred policy is adopted and whose happiness is therefore increased, and some "losers" whose preferred policy is rejected and whose happiness is therefore diminished. There is thus, as [Nobel laureate] Ronald Coase explained, an unavoidable reciprocal harm inherent in any allocation of the right to the indoor air at issue. Adoption of a smoking-permitted policy harms non-smokers, but adoption of a no-smoking policy harms smokers.

In light of this unavoidable, reciprocal harm, social welfare would be maximized if smoking policies were set to favor the group whose total happiness would be most enhanced by implementation of its favored policy. So, if smoking customers value the right to smoke in a particular place more than nonsmoking customers value the right to be free from such smoke, that place should allow smoking. Conversely, if nonsmoking patrons value an establishment's clean air more than smoking patrons value the right to light up, the establishment should ban smoking.

It should thus be clear why a laissez-faire approach of permitting establishment owners to set their own smoking policies will create more welfare than a ban on smoking in public places. Under the laissez-faire approach, a business owner, seeking to maximize his or her profits, will set the establishment's smoking policy to accommodate the patrons who most value their preferred policy (and thus are most willing to pay a premium to be in the proprietor's space). This will result in a variety of smoking policies at different establishments, as business owners respond to the preferences of their customers.

Under a smoking ban, by contrast, business owners are not permitted to cater to smoking patrons' demands even when those patrons value the right to smoke more than nonsmoking patrons (and employees) value the right to be free from smoke. A smoking ban, then, is less likely to maximize social welfare than a laissez-faire approach, which ensures that the right to any particular public place's air is allocated to the group that values it most.

Arguments for Bans Are Weak

Government-imposed smoking bans are unwise. Considered closely, the arguments used to justify them falter. The externality argument fails because indoor smoking creates, at worst, a pecuniary externality that will be mitigated by the price mechanism. Preference-shaping arguments are weak because heavy-handed government restrictions create a substantial risk of "norm backlash." Risk-based arguments are insufficient because the slight risks associated with ETS cannot justify the substantial privacy intrusion occasioned by sweeping smoking bans. In the end, a laissez-faire policy that would permit private business owners to tailor their own smoking policies according to the demands of their patrons is most likely to maximize social welfare by providing an optimal allocation of both smoking and smoke-free establishments.

> "We should not readily agree to be held captive in a halfway house erected by an inadequate assessment of the demands of liberty."

Unrestrained Smoking Impinges on Human Freedom

Amartya Sen

Amartya Sen is a Lamont University professor at Harvard University and received the 1998 Nobel Prize for economics. In the following viewpoint, Sen charges that arguments against smoking bans tend to fall apart in their vagueness when it comes to defining the harmed parties. While passive smokers and nonsmokers have been taken into account, affected individuals not currently in the scope of recorded statistics should also include the future selves of the smokers, who in their youth may not be properly equipped to make shrewd behavioral choices until more life experience has granted them the necessary wisdom.

As you read, consider the following questions:

1. Why are debates about the validity of smoking statistics in policy-making a matter of personal "nostalgia" for the author?

2. In the author's view, what faulty logic does Martin Wolf employ in his statement about intervention on personal liberty requiring "costs proportionate to likely gains"?

3. How does the author justify sharing the costs of public services to treat former smokers with medical problems?

Proposals, including those in Britain and France, for fairly draconian bans on smoking in public places have caused much anger and protest. This is as it should be, since the issue is controversial. But the contrary arguments demand critical scrutiny. One line of critique questions the use of statistical evidence for policymaking. Another invokes the importance of liberty to do what one likes in one's own life.

David Hockney, the distinguished artist, has argued that he has read "all their statistics" about the connection between smoking and disease, but he must observe that "fate plays part in life, that mysterious forces are at work on life": "Medical statisticians cannot grasp this, but almost everyone else does." What, then, should we make of such foundational doubts about the relevance of statistical reasoning?

This is, in fact, nostalgic territory for me personally. As a young student at Cambridge in the 1950s, I listened with rapt attention to Professor R.A. Fisher, perhaps the leading statistical theorist of his time, questioning the use by Richard Doll, the renowned medical scientist, of statistical evidence linking smoking with cancer. I was fascinated by the debate for many different reasons, not the least of which was the thoroughly personal one that I *did* smoke for four years from the age of 14 (it seemed to me, then, to be a very reasonable gesture of defiance) but ended up with cancer of the mouth when I was just 18 (I was lucky enough to get by with massive radiational treatment in Calcutta, though not without some long-lasting penalties).

Of course, my own experience may well have been a fluke and certainly just one case would prove nothing. But I do not see how we can rely on invoking "mysterious forces" and ignore arguments based on assessments of likelihood (Fisher, in fact, offered a different explanation of the observed connection, which proved unsustainable).

Should Smokers Be "Free" to Harm Themselves?

As far as public policy goes, group statistics can still be used to predict group results with some degree of certainty. It has been estimated by public health experts such as Professor Prabhat Jha and his colleagues that more than five million premature deaths per year are currently connected with the use of tobacco. Unless smoking trends change, there would be about 150 million tobacco-related deaths in the first quarter of this century, which would rise to 300 million in the second quarter.

A seemingly more plausible argument, based on the value of freedom, has been presented against smoking bans by [economist] Martin Wolf. People have the right to do what they like with their own lives. While there is possible harm from breathing in smoke from others ("passive smoking"), that is not in itself decisive. Mr. Wolf argued that while "harm to others is a necessary justification" for interfering with liberty, "it is not sufficient." "Intervention should also be," he went on to argue, "both effective and carry costs proportionate to likely gains."

I agree with Mr. Wolf that freedom is centrally important. But how should we see the demands of freedom when habit-forming behavior today restricts the freedom of the same person in the future? Once acquired, the habit of smoking is hard to kick, and it can be asked, with some plausibility, whether youthful smokers have an unqualified right to place their future selves in such bondage.

A similar issue was addressed by the leading apostle of liberty, John Stuart Mill, when he argued against a person's freedom to sell himself or herself in slavery. Mill concluded his discussion of this issue, in *On Liberty*, by noting: "The principle of freedom cannot require that the person be free not to be free," and that "it is not freedom to be allowed to alienate his freedom." Mill's principle may demand more discussion, but it is important that the practical case for tobacco control is not dismissed on the basis of an incomplete libertarian argument.

Another question to ask is: who exactly are the "others" who are affected? Passive smokers are not the only people who might be harmed. If smokers are made ill by their decision to go on smoking, then the society can either take the view that these victims of self-choice have no claim to public resources (such as the National Health Service or social safety nets), or more leniently (and I believe more reasonably) it could accept that these people still qualify to get social help. If the former, we would live in a monstrously unforgiving society; and happily I do not see Britain or France going that way. If the latter, then the interests of "others" would surely be affected through the sharing of the costs of public services.

Libertarian logic for non-interference, when consistently explored, can have extraordinarily stern implications in invalidating the right to assistance from the society when one is hit by self-harming behaviour. If that annulment is not accepted, then the case for libertarian "immunity" from interference is also correspondingly undermined.

We should not readily agree to be held captive in a halfway house erected by an inadequate assessment of the demands of liberty.

> "When it comes to how people feel about
> their lives, they may well prefer to make
> their own bad choices rather than have
> better ones imposed on them."

Government's Intervention on Health Issues Impinges on Freedoms

Jacob Sullum

Jacob Sullum is the author of For Your Own Good: The Anti-Smoking Crusade and the Tyranny of Public Health. *In the following viewpoint, he claims that smoking bans are an insidious outgrowth of government's efforts to control and ostracize forms of human behavior. Sullum states that the "nanny state" is a uniquely modern phenomenon that has partly come about, ironically, as a response to the successful eradication of infectious diseases that are no longer a threat. These attempts by physicians to make people "virtuous" rather than treat the "consequences of their vices," could not, in Sullum's estimation, be in more striking opposition to American ideals of personal liberty and limited government interference in the personal choices of its populace.*

As you read, consider the following questions:

1. How does the author use a quote from John Stuart Mill's

1859 book, *On Liberty*, to illustrate his point that smoking bans are an abuse of power by the government?

2. In the author's view, how is the national prevention strategy adopted by the US Centers for Disease Control and Prevention "a classic example of bureaucratic empire building"?

3. In the author's view, what are the differences, and tradeoffs, between maximizing health and maximizing happiness?

In February [2007], upon introducing the Family Smoking Prevention and Tobacco Control Act, Rep. Henry Waxman (D-Calif.) said the legislation "would give FDA broad powers to regulate tobacco products and protect public health."

In 2004 Sen. Hillary Clinton (D-N.Y.) urged us to think about children's entertainment "from a public health perspective." In that light, she said, "exposing our children to so much of this unchecked media is a kind of contagion," a "silent epidemic" that threatens "long-term public health damage to many, many children and therefore to society."

In 2003 Surgeon General Richard Carmona, declaring that "obesity has reached epidemic proportions," offered "a *simple* prescription that can end America's obesity epidemic": "Every American needs to eat healthy food in healthy portions and be physically active every day."

In 1999 Thom White Wolf Fassett, general secretary of the United Methodist General Board of Church and Society, applauded the work of the National Gambling Impact Study Commission, saying its report "uncovers the hidden epidemic of gambling addiction." Later that year, two addiction specialists, David Korn and Howard Shatter, published a paper in the *Journal of Gambling Studies* calling for "a public health perspective towards gambling."

What do these four "public health" problems—smoking, playing violent video games, overeating, and gambling—have in common? They're all things that some people enjoy and other people condemn, attributing to them various bad effects. Sometimes these effects are medical, but they may also be psychological, behavioral, social, or financial. Calling the habits that supposedly lead to these consequences "public health" problems, "epidemics" that need to be controlled, equates choices with diseases, disguises moralizing as science, and casts meddling as medicine. It elevates a collectivist calculus of social welfare above the interests of individuals, who become subject to increasingly intrusive interventions aimed at making them as healthy as they can be, without regard to their own preferences.

This tendency to call every perceived problem affecting more than two people an "epidemic" obscures a crucial distinction. The classic targets of public health were risks imposed on people against their will, communicable diseases being the paradigmatic example. The more recent targets are risks that people voluntarily assume, such as those associated with smoking, drinking, eating junk food, exercising too little, watching TV too much, playing poker, owning a gun, driving a car without wearing a seat belt, or riding a bicycle without wearing a helmet. The difference is the one John Stuart Mill urged in his 1859 book *On Liberty*: "The sole end for which mankind are warranted, individually or collectively, in interfering with the liberty of action of any of their number is self-protection. . . .The only purpose for which power can be rightfully exercised over any member of a civilized community, against his will, is to prevent harm to others. His own good, either physical or moral, is not a sufficient warrant." Mill's "harming principle" is obviously important to libertarians, but public health practitioners also should keep it in mind if they do not want to be seen as moralistic busybodies constantly seeking to expand the reach of government.

Under Mill's principle, there is a strong case for government intervention to prevent the spread of a deadly microbe, extending even to such highly coercive measures as forcible quarantine or legally mandated medication. The case for intervention to prevent people from placing bets, eating ice cream, or playing *Grand Theft Auto* is much weaker. It requires demonstrating that such activities harm not only the people engaged in them but other people as well. And although Mill was imprecise on this point in *On Liberty*, harm to others has to be understood as a necessary but not sufficient condition for government intervention. To justify the use of force, the alleged harm has to be the sort that the government has a duty to prevent—that is, the sort that violates people's rights.

The Transformation of Public Health

Public health used to mean keeping statistics, imposing quarantines, requiring vaccination of children, providing purified water, building sewer systems, inspecting restaurants, regulating emissions from factories, and reviewing medicines for safety. Nowadays it means, among other things, banning cigarette ads, raising alcohol taxes, restricting gun ownership, forcing people to buckle their seat belts, redesigning cities to discourage driving, and making illegal drug users choose between prison and "treatment." In the past, public health officials could argue that they were protecting people from external threats: carriers of contagious diseases, fumes from the local glue factory, contaminated water, food poisoning, dangerous quack remedies. By contrast, the new enemies of public health come from within; the aim is to protect people from themselves—from their own carelessness, shortsightedness, weak will, or bad values—rather than from each other.

Although this sweeping approach is a relatively recent development, we can find intimations of it in the public health rhetoric of the 19th century. In the introduction to the first major American book on public health, U.S. Army surgeon John Shaw Billings explained the field's concerns: "Whatever can cause, or help to cause, discomfort, pain, sickness, death, vice, or crime— and whatever has a tendency to avert, destroy, or diminish such causes—are matters of interest to the sanitarian." Despite this ambitious mandate, and despite the book's impressive length (nearly 1,500 pages in two volumes), *A Treatise on Hygiene and Public Health* had little to say about the issues that occupy today's public health professionals. There were no sections on smoking, alcoholism, drug abuse, obesity, vehicular accidents, mental illness, suicide, homicide, domestic violence, or unwanted pregnancy. Published in 1879, the book was instead concerned with things like compiling vital statistics, preventing the spread of disease, abating public nuisances, and assuring wholesome food, clean drinking water, and sanitary living conditions.

A century later, public health textbooks were discussing the control of communicable diseases mainly as history. The field's present and future lay elsewhere. "The entire spectrum of 'social ailments,' such as drug abuse, venereal disease, mental illness, suicide, and accidents, includes problems appropriate to public health activity," explained *Principles of Community Health* in 1977. "The greatest potential for improving the health of the American people is to be found in what they do and don't do to and for themselves. Individual decisions about diet, exercise, stress, and smoking are of critical importance." Similarly, the 1978 edition of *Introduction to Public Health* noted that the field, which once "had much narrower interests," now "includes the *social and behavioral aspects of life*—endangered by contemporary stresses, addictive diseases, and emotional instability." (Emphasis in the original.)

In a sense, the change in focus is understandable. After all, Americans are not dying the way they once did. The chapter on infant mortality in *A Treatise on Hygiene and Public Health* reports that during the late 1860s and early 1870s two-fifths to one-half of children in major American cities died before reaching the age of 5. The major killers included measles, scarlet fever, smallpox, diphtheria, whooping cough, bronchitis, pneumonia, tuberculosis, and "diarrheal diseases." Beginning in the 1870s, the discovery that infectious diseases were caused by specific microorganisms made it possible to control them through vaccination, antibiotics, better sanitation, water purification, and elimination of rats, mosquitoes, and other carriers. At the same time, improvements in nutrition and living conditions increased resistance to infection.

Americans no longer live in terror of smallpox or cholera. Despite occasional outbreaks of infectious diseases such as rabies and tuberculosis, the fear of epidemics that was once an accepted part of life is virtually unknown. The one major exception is AIDS, which is not readily transmitted and remains largely confined to a few high-risk groups. For the most part, Americans are dying of things you can't catch: cancer, heart disease, trauma. Accordingly, the public health establishment is focusing on those causes and the factors underlying them. Having vanquished most true epidemics, it has turned its attention to metaphorical "epidemics" of unhealthy behavior.

Birth of a Revolution

In 1979 Surgeon General Julius Richmond released *Healthy People: The Surgeon General's Report on Health Promotion and Disease Prevention*, which broke new ground by setting specific goals for reductions in mortality. In the introduction, Joseph Califano, then secretary of the Department of Health, Education, and Welfare, warned that "we are killing ourselves by our own careless habits" and called for "a second public health revolution" (the first being the triumph over infectious diseases). *Healthy People*, which estimated that "perhaps as much as half of U.S. mortality in 1976 was due to unhealthy behavior or lifestyle," advised Americans to quit smoking, drink less, exercise more, fasten their seat belts, stop driving so fast, and cut down on fat, salt, and sugar. It also recommended motorcycle helmet laws and gun control.

Healthy People drew on a "national prevention strategy" developed by what is now the U.S. Centers for Disease Control and Prevention (CDC). Established during World War II as a unit of the U.S. Public Health Service charged with fighting malaria in the South, the CDC today includes eight different centers, only two of which deal with the control of infectious disease. The National Center for Chronic Disease Prevention and Health Promotion, for example, includes the Office on Smoking and Health and the Division of Nutrition and Physical Activity.

The CDC's growth can be seen as a classic example of bureaucratic empire building. Although it is easy to dismiss public health's ever-expanding agenda as a bid for funding, power, and status, the field's practitioners argue with evident sincerity that they are simply adapting to changing patterns of morbidity and mortality. In doing so, however, they are treating behavior as if it were a communicable disease, which obscures some important distinctions. Contrary to the impression left by all the warnings about a "methamphetamine epidemic" that is supposedly sweeping the country, or by CDC maps that show obesity spreading like a plague from state to state, behavior cannot be transmitted to other people against their will. People do not choose to be sick, but they do choose to engage in risky behavior. The choice implies that the behavior, unlike a viral or bacterial infection, has value. It also implies that attempts to control the behavior will be resisted.

The Right to Unhealthy Choices

Healthy People noted that "formidable obstacles" stand in the way of improved public health. "Prominent among them are individual attitudes toward the changes necessary for better health," it said. "Though opinion polls note greater interest in healthier lifestyles, many people remain apathetic and unmotivated. . . . Some consider activities to promote health moralistic rather than scientific; still others are wary of measures which they feel may infringe on personal liberties. However, the scientific basis for suggested measures has grown so compelling, it is likely that such biases will begin to shift." In other words, people engage in risky behavior because they don't know any better. Once they realize the risks they are taking, they will change their ways.

Surely there is a measure of truth to this. The publicity surrounding the first surgeon general's report on the health hazards of smoking, published in 1964, was followed by a more or less steady decline in the prevalence of smoking among Americans, from 42 percent of adults in 1965 to about half that today. Some of that decline, especially in recent years, probably has been due to coercive measures such as smoking bans and cigarette tax hikes, but most of it was seen in the first couple of decades, when the main tactics of the anti-smoking movement were education and persuasion. Likewise, the dramatic increase in seat belt use by Americans, from 15 percent of drivers and front-seat passengers in 1984 to 80 percent two decades later, may have been partly due to the threat of fines, but greater awareness of the safety benefits also has played an important role.

Still, some people, even after they understand the risks they're taking, obstinately continue to take them. To Richard Carmona, it may be obvious that "every American needs to eat healthy food in healthy portions and be physically active every day." But what if some Americans, or many, or most, refuse to get with the program?

An Unspoken Moral Premise

As early as June 1975, in its *Forward Plan for Health*, the U.S. Public Health Service was suggesting "strong regulations to control the advertisement of food products, especially those of high sugar content or little nutritional value." Since then, as Americans have gotten fatter, calls for restrictions on ads, especially those aimed at children, have intensified. Anti-fat crusaders such as the Yale obesity expert Kelly Brownell are pushing "junk food" taxes to discourage consumption of cheeseburgers and potato chips, along with subsidies to encourage consumption of fruits and vegetables. You could extend that idea to the energy expenditure side of the equation, taxing products associated with sloth, such as books and TV sets, and subsidizing products associated with exercise, such as bicycles and treadmills. Other proposals include lawsuits to compel restaurant menu changes, bans on fast food near schools, and an "equal time" rule requiring stations that air ads for fast food and sugary breakfast cereals to carry propaganda urging people to eat better and exercise more.

None of this is likely to work. There is little evidence that kids like candy and ice cream, or eat more of it, because of advertising; that they see more food advertising now than they did when they were thinner; or that bans on ads aimed at children, which have been imposed in Sweden and Quebec [Canada], make kids slimmer. The price control system envisioned by Kelly Brownell and like-minded activists raises insoluble calculation problems, and since tax rates would be the same for every buyer, it would either overdeter moderate eaters or underdeter gluttons—probably both. Restaurants can sell only what people are willing to eat, and litigation will not change that. Establishing fast-food-free zones near schools would not prevent students from bringing their own fattening food to school, and it would not affect most of their meals in any case. And even if a policy of forcing stations to carry anti-obesity messages survived a First Amendment challenge (which it wouldn't), it is doubtful that telling people what they already know—that exercise and a balanced diet are important to good health—would have much of an impact.

But I can think of a couple of policies that would make a difference. Instead of a "junk food" tax, which is inefficient and unfair because it is paid by the thin as well as the fat, why not tax people for every pound over their ideal weight? People would be required to get weighed once a year at an approved station, which would send its report to the Internal Revenue Service. If the tax were set high enough, I'm sure many people would lose weight. If that seems too complicated, how about mandatory calisthenics in the town square every morning? Assuming these policies are feasible and cost-effective, is there any basis for objecting to them "from a public health perspective"?

If not, I'd suggest that the public health perspective leaves out some important considerations. Maximizing health is not the same as maximizing happiness. The public health mission to minimize morbidity and mortality leaves no room for the possibility that someone might accept a shorter life span, or an increased risk of disease or injury, in exchange for more pleasure or less discomfort. Motorcyclists, rock climbers, and sky divers make that sort of decision all the time, and not all of them are ignorant of the relevant injury and fatality statistics. With lifestyle choices that pose longer-term risks, such as smoking and overeating, the dangers may be easier to ignore, but it is still possible for someone with a certain set of tastes and preferences to say, "Let me enjoy myself now; I'll take my chances." The assumption that such tradeoffs are unacceptable is the unspoken moral premise of public health. When the surgeon general declares that "every American needs to eat healthy food in healthy portions and be physically active every day," where does that leave a guy who prefers to be fat if it means he can eat what he likes and relax in his spare time instead of looking for ways to burn calories?

The "Right" Choices

It's true that, as the anti-smoking activist William Cahan pointed out on a CNN talk show several years ago, "People who are making decisions for themselves don't always come up with the right answer." They don't necessarily make tradeoffs between health and other values in an informed or carefully considered manner. Sometimes they regret their decisions. But they know their own tastes and preferences, and they have access to myriad pieces of local information about the relevant costs and benefits that no government regulator can possibly know. They will not always make good decisions, but on balance they will make better decisions, as measured by their own subsequent evaluations, than any third party deciding for them. Leaving aside the question of who is better positioned to decide whether a given pleasure is worth the risk associated with it, there is an inherent value to freedom: When it comes to how people feel about their lives, they may well prefer to make their own bad choices rather than have better ones imposed on them.

Needless to say, people make mistakes—sometimes expensive, hard-to-correct mistakes—in many areas of life. If that fact is reason enough for the government to second-guess their decisions about dangerous activities such as smoking cigarettes and riding motorcycles, why on earth should the government let people make their own choices when it comes to such consequential matters as where to live, how much education to get, whom to marry, whether to have children, which job to take, or what religion to practice? These decisions are at least as important, and the government is at least as well equipped to make them as it is to decide which health risks are acceptable.

While people are not perfect judges of their own interests, they are better judges, by and large, than government officials are apt to be. That is the utilitarian case against paternalism and in favor of individual freedom. But what if people making health-related decisions are not truly free? Some paternalists claim that surrendering to certain habits, such as drug use or gambling, is akin to selling yourself into slavery, which Mill himself said was not an acceptable use of freedom.

It's pretty clear from Mill's condemnation of alcohol prohibition that he did not share this view of addiction. In any case, there is abundant evidence that addiction is a pattern of behavior shaped by a complex interaction of personal and situational variables, not an automatic process in which people become "hooked" without regard to their own choices or desires. In that sense it is quite different from being clapped in chains and forced to follow another person's commands.

Mill also made an exception for minors, of course; and so-called public health threats, such as the violent entertainment that vexes Hillary Clinton, are often described as menaces to children. People who oppose paternalism vis-à-vis adults can nevertheless support measures, such as a legally enforced cigarette purchase age, that are narrowly targeted at preventing minors from making risky decisions that are properly reserved for grownups. But child protection often becomes an excuse for restricting the freedom of adults. The aforementioned fast-food-free zones, for example, probably would not make kids noticeably thinner but certainly would make life harder for adults looking for a quick and convenient lunch while working or running errands near schools.

Sometimes politicians and activists who claim to be fighting for parents are actually complaining about the appalling stuff that parents let their kids see, do, or eat. They want to override parental prerogatives instead of reinforcing them. Sen. Clinton, for example, worries that parents do not make enough use of the "V chip" her husband championed as a way to prevent children from seeing inappropriate TV shows. But perhaps they simply are not as alarmed as she is about the state of popular culture. Likewise, activists who want to ban food marketing aimed at children do not seem to trust parents to say no when their kids demand SpongeBob SquarePants Pop-Tarts or Dora the Explorer cookies. . . .

The Corruption of Medicine by Morality

Because the public health field developed in response to deadly threats that spread from person to person and place to place, its practitioners are used to enlisting the state in their cause. Writing in 1879, John Shaw Billings put it this way: "All admit that the State should extend special protection to those who are incapable of judging of their own best interests, or of taking care of themselves, such as the insane, persons of feeble intellect, or children; and we have seen that in sanitary matters the public at large are thus incompetent."

Billings was defending measures aimed at traditional public health targets, such as infectious diseases and toxic pollution. It's reasonable to expect that such efforts will be welcomed by the intended beneficiaries once they understand the aim. The same cannot be said of public health's new targets. Even after the public is informed about the relevant hazards, many people will continue to behave in ways frowned upon by the public health establishment. This is not because they misunderstood; it's because, for the sake of pleasure, utility, or convenience, they are prepared to accept the risks. When public health experts assume these decisions are wrong, they do indeed treat adults like children.

One such expert, Boston public health official Leon S. White, reflected on the recalcitrance of risktakers in 1975, the year the federal government published its *Forward Plan for Health*, which set forth a "prevention strategy" that included various laws aimed at stopping people from harming themselves. "The real malpractice problem in this country today," White wrote in *The New England Journal of Medicine*, "is not the one described on the front pages of daily newspapers but rather the malpractice that people are performing on themselves and each other. . . . It is a crime to commit suicide quickly. However, to kill oneself slowly by means of an unhealthy life style is readily condoned and even encouraged." White's article prompted a response from Robert Meenan, a professor at the University of California School of Medicine in San Francisco, who observed: "Health professionals . . . have no personal attributes, knowledge, or training that qualifies them to dictate the preferences of others. Nevertheless, doctors generally assume that the high priority that they place on health should be shared by others. They find it hard to accept that some people may opt for a brief, intense existence full of unhealthy practices. Such individuals are pejoratively labeled 'noncompliant' and pressures are applied on them to reorder their priorities."

This is what H.L. Mencken had in mind when he remarked that "hygiene is the corruption of medicine by morality. It is impossible to find a hygienist who does not debase his theory of the healthful with a theory of the virtuous. The whole hygienic art, indeed, resolves itself into an ethical exhortation. This brings it, at the end, into diametrical conflict with medicine proper.

The true aim of medicine is not to make men virtuous; it is to safeguard and rescue them from the consequences of their vices. The physician does not preach repentance; he offers absolution." Whether or not you agree with Mencken's view of the physician's proper role, the danger of transforming a doctor's orders into the government's orders should be clear.

"Health for All"

But not to everyone. Some public health theorists explicitly recognize that their aims are fundamentally collectivist and cannot be reconciled with the American tradition of limited government. In 1975 Dan Beauchamp, then an assistant professor of public health at the University of North Carolina, presented a paper at the annual meeting of the American Public Health Association in which he argued that "the radical individualism inherent in the market model" is the biggest obstacle to improving public health. "The historic dream of public health that preventable death and disability ought to be minimized is a dream of social justice," Beauchamp said. "We are far from recognizing the principle that death and disability are collective problems and that all persons are entitled to health protection."

Not only are all persons entitled to health protection, but they're going to get it, whether they want it or not. Beauchamp rejected "the ultimately arbitrary distinction between voluntary and involuntary hazards" and complained that "the primary duty to avert disease and injury still rests with the individual." He called upon public health practitioners to challenge "the powerful sway market-justice holds over our imagination, granting fundamental freedom to all individuals to be left alone." So the right to be left alone—the right Supreme Court Justice Louis Brandeis considered "the most comprehensive of rights and the right most valued by civilized men"—turns out to be the leading risk factor for disease and injury.

Beauchamp may be unusually candid, but his vision is implicit in the way public health is currently understood. According to

John Hanlon's *Public Health Administration and Practice*, "public health is dedicated to the common attainment of the highest levels of physical, mental, and social well-being and longevity consistent with available knowledge and resources at a given time and place." The textbook *Principles of Community Health* tells us that "the most widely accepted definition of individual health is that of the World Health Organization [WHO]: 'Health is a state of complete physical, mental, and social well-being and not merely the absence of disease or infirmity.'" Especially in light of this definition, the WHO's goal of "Health for All," if it is meant to be a prescription for state action, has a chilling sound to it.

"Over himself, over his own body and mind, the individual is sovereign," Mill insisted. The mandate "Health for All" replaces that principle with a legally enforceable duty to be well, a demand by the collective to keep one's body and mind in optimal condition. A government empowered to maximize health is a not a government under which anyone who values liberty would want to live.

| "An increase in the tobacco levy simply
makes sense."

Cigarette Taxes Benefit Society as a Whole

Rachel Kaprielian and Herman Hamilton

Rachel Kaprielian is a former Massachusetts state representative and sponsor of tobacco-tax legislation. Reverend Herman Hamilton is president of the Greater Boston Interfaith Organization. Kaprielian and Hamilton, the authors of the following viewpoint, contend that raising tobacco taxes is both wise fiscal policy and an effective deterrent that helps prevent youths from taking up smoking. They note that in states like Michigan and Alaska, where such levies have been imposed, revenues have increased while the number of deaths attributable to smoking-related diseases have correspondingly declined.

As you read, consider the following questions:

1. What are the two principal reasons cited by the authors that make raising tobacco taxes beneficial to the state?
2. How do the authors respond to pronouncements by critics that raising the tobacco tax would push people to buy products in other states that tax less?

3. In the authors' view, how does raising the tobacco tax save money statewide?

Each year, as the [Massachusetts] Legislature sets the state budget, members are confronted with making tough and balanced choices while remaining steadfast to sound public policy. Nowhere is that more evident than in the state's commitment to ensuring the success of its landmark healthcare reform law, an initiative that is providing insurance to the uninsured but carries with it a price tag of nearly $400 million in fiscal year 2009.

Now is not the time to backtrack on the law, a national model that other states are working to emulate. A basic component to this success is in its inclusion of prevention measures that seek to improve the overall public health—today and down the road.

Cigarette smoking is the leading cause of preventable death and disease in Massachusetts. Twenty-five people die each day in the state from tobacco-related illnesses, and thousands of others suffer from related ailments—emphysema, heart disease, cancer—many unable to work or enjoy quality of life. Its wrath results in great personal, physical, societal, and fiscal cost. To combat this reality requires a multi-faceted and fiscally responsible approach: one that brings in needed revenue while adding immeasurable benefits toward prevention and cessation of smoking. Currently, there is a legislative proposal that would add $1 to the levy on cigarettes. Its passage would add about $150 million to state coffers, which would enable the Legislature to continue healthcare reform, as well as reduce the incidence of smoking rates overall. Data shows that for every 10 percent increase in the cost of a pack of cigarettes, the overall smoking rates decrease 4 percent.

Perhaps more compelling, raising the price of smoking will discourage children, who are still the tobacco companies' main target, from picking up the habit in the first place. That will lower future healthcare costs and help break the cycle of addiction. A leading study shows that nearly every adult who smokes (almost

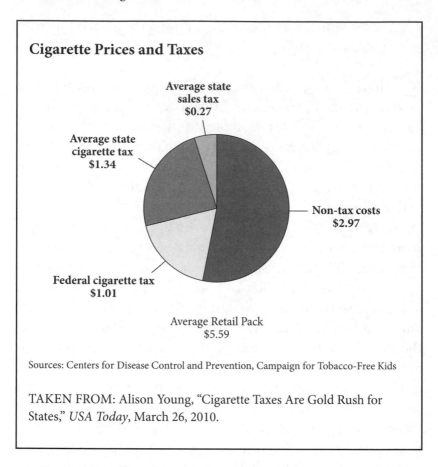

Cigarette Prices and Taxes

Average state
sales tax
$0.27

Average state
cigarette tax
$1.34

Non-tax costs
$2.97

Federal cigarette tax
$1.01

Average Retail Pack
$5.59

Sources: Centers for Disease Control and Prevention, Campaign for Tobacco-Free Kids

TAKEN FROM: Alison Young, "Cigarette Taxes Are Gold Rush for States," *USA Today*, March 26, 2010.

90 percent) took his or her first puff at or before age 18. If passed, this legislation would translate into 46,000 fewer future kid smokers coupled with 25,000 fewer adult smokers.

Every year, Massachusetts spends over $3.5 billion to treat sick smokers. These are critical dollars that could be spent on other health priorities, prevention programs, or other important needs in our state.

Raising the Tobacco Tax Saves Money

Critics of the increase say that it will push sales to states that tax less. They also say it is a regressive tax that will dwindle over time. Neither is true. Convenience stores in border towns

IS THIS THE SMOKING AREA?

"Is this the smoking area?" cartoon by Ralph Hagen, www.CartoonStock.com. Copyright © Ralph Hagen. Reproduction rights obtainable from www.CartoonStock.com.

noticed a slight dip in business after past increases, but, over time, found that buyers returned. This makes sense [because] cigarettes, like gum, candy, and soda, are typically purchases of convenience.

And other states, most notably Michigan and Alaska, have found that even with an increase in the cigarette tax, their revenues have steadily increased, not decreased.

But raising the tobacco tax saves money here too. The child with asthma whose parent stops smoking today will have fewer asthma-related complications from secondhand smoke tomorrow. An expectant mother encouraged to kick the habit by higher prices will give birth to a healthier baby. The teenager who doesn't start smoking becomes the adult with fewer chances of getting lung cancer, emphysema, or chronic heart disease.

And from a strict fiscal analysis, it would save the state over $1 billion in long-term healthcare costs.

So an increase in the tobacco levy simply makes sense. It deters children from smoking. It helps taxpayers, heathcare providers, hospitals, and insurance ratepayers. And it extends a helping hand to those hard-pressed families and individuals who are working but lack health insurance.

> *"So-called 'sin taxes' are a moral hazard for government because they begin as an attempt to discourage 'undesirable' behavior and quickly end up being a 'necessary' source of funding for unrelated government programs and services."*

Cigarette Taxes Punish the Wrong People

Bruce Smith and Kathryn Hickok

Bruce Smith is the author of Tobacco Revenues Prove Addictive. *Kathryn Hickok is publications director at the Cascade Policy Institute, a think tank based in Portland, Oregon. In the following viewpoint, Smith and Hickok maintain that raising cigarette taxes unfairly punishes smokers. The increased revenues produced by raising cigarette taxes wind up subsidizing other projects that have little or nothing to do with smoking prevention programs. Additionally, the authors claim, those living at or below the poverty line bear the brunt of the costs, since they are statistically likelier to be smokers.*

As you read, consider the following questions:

Bruce Smith and Kathryn Hickok, "Warning: 'Sin Taxes' May Be Hazardous to the State," *Cascade Commentary*, October 2006. www.cascadepolicy.org. Copyright © 2006 by the Cascade Policy Institute. All rights reserved. Reproduced by permission.

1. How do the authors refute claims by politicians that raising Oregon's cigarette tax would save future unfunded state health care costs?
2. What pattern of Oregon's smoking demographic do the authors find fiscally unjust and why?
3. In the authors' view, how has Oregon "created a tremendous moral hazard" by using funds from cigarette taxes and the tobacco companies' Master Settlement Agreement to pay for health care, education, and law enforcement?

On September 25, 2006, during his campaign for reelection, Governor Ted Kulongoski proposed raising Oregon's cigarette tax by nearly 85 cents (bringing the total tax per pack to $2.025) to help expand health coverage for uninsured children under the Oregon Health Plan. While some politicians find this source of revenue appealing, a "moral hazard" is always inevitable when "sin taxes" are used to fund state services.

So-called "sin taxes" are a moral hazard for government because they begin as an attempt to discourage "undesirable" behavior and quickly end up being a "necessary" source of funding for unrelated government programs and services. Oregon's $1.18 per pack cigarette tax is a prime example. Using a cigarette tax to combat smoking and to raise revenue for state programs and services, as the State of Oregon claims to be attempting, is not possible. These are two mutually exclusive goals: for one to succeed, the other must fail.

Many Oregonians probably assume that cigarette taxes recoup state health care costs generated by smoking-related illnesses and fund anti-smoking and smoking cessation programs. In reality, the 20% of the population who smoke cigarettes are both disproportionately and regressively taxed to fund services completely unrelated to smoking.

Many politicians justify Oregon's cigarette tax by claiming that each pack of cigarettes will end up generating several dollars'

The Inherent Conflict of Sin Taxes

On occasion, "sin taxes" are defended because supposedly they both raise revenue and discourage the use of the sinful product. As John Bloom, the American Cancer Society's policy director said, "Canada has proven that tobacco taxes save lives and raise revenue." But one might ask whether a collision course is imminent here. Sin taxes do not raise revenue unless people use the product, and they do not save lives unless people avoid the product. Will not many of those who want to raise the revenue want people to commit the sin of using the product?

James A. Sadowsky, "The Economics of Sin Taxes," AnthonyFlood.com.

worth of future unfunded state health care costs. However, estimates vary, and quotes have ranged from four dollars per pack to as much as $12.70. Not only are the numbers inconsistent, but they are misleading. Many negative economic impacts of smoking are actually borne by smokers themselves, not by the government. Such studies fail to take into account many factors which nearly cancel out the future cost of a pack of cigarettes to the state.

Tax Revenue Is Not Funding Smoking Prevention

Whatever future costs may or may not be borne by the state, Oregon smokers are not simply being forced to pay for their own health care. $55 million of cigarette tax revenue in 2005 paid for services such as education, law enforcement and light rail. These services have nothing to do with smoking or smokers' health care.

Due to the demographics of the smoking population, smokers are regressively taxed to fund these general services. Those living below the poverty line are about 50% more likely to smoke than those living above it. Therefore, Oregon's poorest citizens are more likely than other Oregonians to pay the tax.

While politicians maintain they would like to see smoking eradicated, the truth is that if everyone in Oregon were to quit smoking, the state would lose a steady stream of revenue and be left with a yearly $288 million budget gap. When asked to comment on a proposed cigarette tax increase to fill budget gaps in 2002, then-gubernatorial-candidate Ted Kulongoski remarked that such an increase would be ineffective because it would only discourage cigarette consumption. Four years later, it appears he has changed his mind.

By using funds from cigarette taxes and the tobacco companies' Master Settlement Agreement (MSA) to pay for health care, education and law enforcement, Oregon has created a tremendous moral hazard. With so many essential state programs dependent on cigarette taxes, it has become in the state's interest to keep smokers smoking. By issuing bonds backed by future payments from the MSA, the State of Oregon must see to it that people are smoking years down the road.

Perhaps it is not surprising, then, that one budget area receiving almost no cigarette revenues is smoking prevention. Of the $288 million Oregon received from cigarettes in 2005, only $3.5 million funded anti-smoking programs. This is only 16 percent of what the Centers for Disease Control recommends for an anti-smoking program to be effective.

If Oregon wants to recoup losses incurred by treating smoking-related illnesses and to fully fund a smoking prevention program, a 15-cent tax per pack (in conjunction with continued MSA payments) would more than suffice. Yet, cigarette taxes remain eight times higher and growing, while smoking prevention and cessation programs remain a low priority. If cigarette taxes do not fund programs legitimately linked to the true public costs of smoking, they should be abolished, rather than expanded to fund more and more aspects of a ballooning state budget.

| "Tobacco control is . . . probably the single most cost-effective intervention for adult health in the world."

Global Tobacco Control Would Save Lives

Prabhat Jha

Prabhat Jha is the Canada research chair for the Department of Public Health Sciences at the University of Toronto and the founding director for the Centre for Global Health Research at St. Michael's Hospital. In the following viewpoint, Jha argues that there is a moral imperative to implement tobacco control, based on the significant number of deaths that are caused worldwide by secondhand smoke. Jha points to data released by the World Health Organization showing that this number will reach 10 million a year within the next twenty five years and that tobacco inhalation is the only major and growing cause of preventable death outside of HIV-1. Legislated curbs on tobacco and increases in tobacco taxes in countries such as France and the United Kingdom, he claims, have already been dramatically effective in saving hundreds of million of lives, a priority that vastly outweighs any dubious infringement of personal liberties.

As you read, consider the following questions:

1. In the author's view, what are three steps that have proven effective in other countries at reducing tobacco use and its consequences?

2. What are two reasons cited by the author regarding why tobacco control measures have not been widely implemented in the United States?

3. How does the author rebut what he deems the two major arguments against tobacco control?

A pandemic is brewing in the developing world. We know the symptoms. We know the cause. We even know something about prevention.

Yet this global killer is ripping through the world's poorer countries largely unchecked. Within 25 years, it will be responsible for 10 million deaths a year, according to the World Health Organization (WHO). At least half of these deaths will occur at ages 35 to 69, which translates into a life expectancy loss of about 25 years.

The culprit? Cigarette smoking. The same addiction that became the top preventable cause of death in the US and other Western countries has already made dramatic inroads abroad. In fact, unless something changes soon, we are seeing history repeat itself—a massive uptake in smoking followed by a massive health toll years down the line.

Worldwide, only HIV-1 and tobacco use appear to be large and growing causes of death. Although we do not know how many tens (or even hundreds) of millions may be killed by AIDS, it is more certain that with current smoking patterns, tobacco use will kill about 1 billion people in the 21st century. This is a ten-fold increase over tobacco-related deaths in the 20th century. Most of the tobacco deaths in this century will occur in developing countries.

A high proportion of these deaths will be among the poor: smoking is already more common in poor than rich men worldwide. In Western countries, smoking deaths account for more than half of the difference in adult death rates between rich and poor men. In India, smoking causes about half of tuberculosis deaths—which itself is more common in the poor.

But the Western reality of the last 60 years does not have to become the developing world's future, not with what we know today. We know how to control tobacco. Cessation by the 1.1 billion current smokers is central to meaningful reductions in tobacco deaths over the next few decades. Reduced uptake of smoking by children would yield benefits chiefly after 2050. Tobacco cessation can be highly effective: Sir Richard Doll and Sir Richard Peto's 50-year study of UK physicians shows that those who quit smoking even in their 40s remarkably lowered their risk of death, and those who quit in their 30s had mortality rates close to those of lifelong non-smokers.

The Virtues of Control

Numerous studies worldwide provide robust evidence that tobacco tax increases, timely dissemination of information on the health risks from smoking, restrictions on smoking in public and work places, comprehensive bans on advertising and promotion, and increased access to tobacco cessation therapies are effective in reducing tobacco use and its consequences. Of these, tobacco taxes are singularly effective. A tripling of the world's excise tax would roughly double the price of cigarettes—as has happened in New York City—and would avoid about 3 million deaths each year by 2030. Tobacco control is thus probably the single most cost-effective intervention for adult health in the world.

When tobacco control has been taken seriously (as in the United Kingdom), tobacco deaths have fallen sharply. A useful barometer of control in the West is lung cancer deaths among young adults. Age-standardized male lung cancer rates at ages 35 to 44 per 100,000 in the United Kingdom fell by nearly 80%. In contrast, comparable French male lung cancer rates show the reverse pattern. In France, the increase in smoking occurred some decades later than in the United Kingdom, but declines in smoking began only after 1990. Similarly, a large increase in female lung cancer at young ages was avoided in the United Kingdom, but female lung cancer continues to rise in France.

Highly effective tobacco control measures should be underway in the developing world. But for the most part, they are not. Whereas taxes are about 80% of the street price of cigarettes in Canada, taxes are less than 30% of the street price in India or China. In many countries, taxes on tobacco have fallen, after adjustment for inflation. Only a few countries, notably South Africa, have significantly raised tobacco taxes. Knowledge of the health risks associated with tobacco use—information that drove down demand in the developed world—is insufficient in poor countries. In China, for example, 61% of smokers questioned in 1996 thought tobacco did them "little or no harm."

Ruthless political opposition from the tobacco industry and economic arguments against tobacco control help to explain why control measures are not widely implemented. Spurious economic arguments against tobacco control have been systematically debunked. Reducing the demand for tobacco—through tax and information increases—would not mean unemployment in most countries. Money not spent on tobacco would be spent on other goods and services. Indeed, cities with aggressive tobacco control, such as Dublin and New York, have seen job gains, not losses. Higher cigarette taxes don't cause such drops in demand that the government loses revenue. Quite the contrary, these price hikes lower consumption and raise revenue. A 10% higher tax means about 7% higher revenue. Such funds are precious resources to fight poverty. In China, a 10% higher price would drop consumption by 5% and raise enough revenue to pay for a basic health program for 33 million poor rural Chinese.

The Lessons of History

A commonly heard claim against tobacco control is that if people are not harming others, then governments should not interfere with their individual decisions. This libertarian view is at odds with both common sense and an increasing body of evidence. Most people begin to smoke as children, when short-sightedness and lack of information make rational decisions difficult. By the time child smokers become adults, over 80% of them in developed countries wish they had never started. Recent economic work that incorporates addiction has begun to repudiate two major arguments against tobacco taxation: that the external costs to others are small (since the health costs to smokers are huge), and that cigarette taxes hurt the poor (since the self-control value of higher taxes helps the poor more). Nobel laureate Amartya Sen wisely reminds us that "it is important that the practical case for tobacco control is not dismissed on the basis of an incomplete libertarian argument."

The agenda is clear. Developing countries and international development agencies must take tobacco seriously as the leading killer of adults worldwide. International poverty goals must include reducing tobacco (specifically tracking if adult smokers quit). A worldwide network to monitor this great epidemic and its control must be strengthened. Developing countries must not be dissuaded by the same empty arguments that mired the tobacco control efforts in the West for so long and allowed smoking to be the killer it is here today. There are hopeful signs. WHO's global tobacco control treaty has been signed by most countries, but this now needs to be implemented with specific economic and epidemiological expertise at a country-level. The Michael Bloomberg Foundation has committed $125 million to global tobacco control. Other enlightened souls should follow.

With use of powerful tax and information tools, developing countries can achieve tobacco control (as measured by rapid increases in ex-smoking rates) within a decade. In contrast, it took the US, Canada, and other Western countries nearly three decades to achieve comparable results. Indeed, Poland and Thailand have seen recent increases in adult cessation—likely as a result of advertising restrictions and information on smoking hazards. If the proportion of adults in developing countries who quit smoking increases from about 5% today to 30%–40% by 2020, then some 150–180 million tobacco deaths would be avoided over the next five decades. Half of these lives saved would be in productive middle age, and social inequalities in adult mortality could be halved. Given that control policies deter children from starting, even greater benefits can be expected beyond 2050.

A history of tobacco deaths need not be a destiny of tobacco deaths. We know much more than we did even one decade ago. The only question is whether we will use it.

| "With all of the good intentions in the world, outlawing cigarettes would be just as disastrous as the prohibition on other drugs."

Banning Cigarettes Is Unfeasable

Tony Newman

Tony Newman is communications director for the Drug Policy Alliance. In the following viewpoint, Newman claims that tobacco bans would be yet another misstep in America's failed war on drugs. Making tobacco more difficult to obtain from legal vendors would help make it a black-market commodity like marijuana or cocaine, with all the same shady and dangerous trappings synonymous with the drug war: shootouts, prison terms, and money laundering to name but a few.

As you read, consider the following questions:

1. In what ways does the author claim that smokers are already victims of discrimination?
2. In what ways does the author claim that a tobacco prohibition would be disastrous?
3. In the author's view, what are three areas in which the

public health campaign around cigarettes has been "a model of success"?

Cigarettes kill; 400,000 people die prematurely every year from smoking. When we analyze the harm from drugs, there is no doubt that cigarettes are the worst.

They kill more people than cocaine, heroin, methamphetamine and all other illegal drugs combined.

More than 800,000 people are arrested every year for marijuana, the vast majority for possession, yet all the data from studies that compare the two substances show that cigarettes are more harmful to an individual's health. If we make these other drugs illegal, shouldn't we outlaw the leading killer?

Considering how we deal with less harmful drugs, making cigarettes illegal seems logical. Over the past decade, we have seen, in states from California to New York, increasing restrictions on when and where people can smoke—and even momentum toward tobacco prohibition.

Smoking is banned in bars and restaurants and on some university campuses. People can now be fired from their jobs because they can't give up smoking. We have seen parents denied adoption rights if they smoke. In some cities, it is nearly impossible to smoke anywhere besides your own home.

The Drug Policy Alliance sponsored a Zogby Poll in 2006, and we were shocked to find that 45 percent of those polled supported making cigarettes illegal within the next 10 years. Among 18- to 29-year-olds, it's more than 50 percent.

The Perils of Control

But with all of the good intentions in the world, outlawing cigarettes would be just as disastrous as the prohibition on other drugs. After all, people would still smoke, just as they still use other drugs that are prohibited, from marijuana to cocaine. But now, in addition to the harm of smoking, we would find a whole range of "collateral consequences" that come along with prohibition.

"I'd like to help, pal, but I'm on my way to arrest a guy for violating a 'no smoking' ordinance," cartoon by Rex May Baloo. www.CartoonStock.com. Copyright © Rex May Baloo. Reproduction rights obtainable from www.CartoonStock.com.

A huge number of people who smoke would continue to do so, but now they would be considered criminals. We would have parents promising their kids that they will stop smoking but still sneaking a smoke.

We would have smokers hiding their habit and smoking in alleys and dark corners, afraid of being caught using the illegal substance. We would have cops using precious time and resources to hassle and arrest cigarette smokers. Our prison overcrowding crisis would rise to an unprecedented level with "addicts" and casual cigarette smokers alike getting locked up.

We would have a black market, with outlaws taking the place of delis and supermarkets and stepping in to meet the demand and provide the desired drug.

Instead of buying your cigarettes in a legally sanctioned place, you would have to hit the streets to pick up your fix. The cigarette trade would provide big revenue to "drug dealers," just as illegal drugs do today. There would be shootouts in the streets and killings over the right to sell the prohibited tobacco plant.

We have tried prohibiting cigarettes in some state prisons, like in California, and we have seen that smoking continues, with cigarettes traded illicitly. There is a violent black market that fills the void and leads to unnecessary deaths over access and the inflated profits.

The Common Sense Approach

Luckily, no one is proposing making cigarettes illegal. On the contrary, our public health campaign around cigarettes has been a model of success compared with our results with other prohibited drugs. By placing high taxes on cigarettes, restricting locations where one can smoke and banning certain kinds of advertising, we have seen a significant decline in the number of people who smoke.

Instead of giving teens "reefer madness"-style propaganda, we have treated young people with respect and given them honest education about the harm of cigarettes, and we have been rewarded with fewer young people smoking today than ever before.

Although we should celebrate our success and continue to encourage people to cut back or give up smoking, let's not get carried away and think that prohibition would eliminate smoking.

We need to realize that drugs, from cigarettes to marijuana to alcohol, will always be consumed, whether they are legal or illegal. Although drugs have health consequences and dangers, making them illegal—and keeping them illegal—will only bring additional death and suffering.

Don't just take my word for it. Take it from the news anchor who was called the most trusted man in America, Walter Cronkite.

Here is what he said about prohibition and our war on drugs: "I covered the Vietnam War. I remember the lies that were told, the lives that were lost—and the shock when, 20 years after the war ended, former Defense Secretary Robert S. McNamara admitted he knew it was a mistake all along. . . .

"And I cannot help but wonder how many more lives, and how much more money, will be wasted before another Robert McNamara admits what is plain for all to see: The war on drugs is a failure."

Periodical and Internet Sources Bibliography

The following articles have been selected to supplement the diverse views presented in this chapter.

James R. Carroll	"A New Fight over Tobacco Regulation," *Louisville Courier-Journal*, June 11, 2011.
William V. Corr	"New Guidelines Show Smokers Have More Tools to Quit than Ever, but Elected Officials Must Do More to Help," TobaccoFreeKids.org, May 7, 2008.
Michael Felberbaum	"Cigarette Packs Get Colorful for 'Light' Label Ban," *Komo News*, June 4, 2010.
Robert Gehrke	"Lawmakers OK $1 Per Pack Cigarette Tax Hike," *Salt Lake Tribune*, March 5, 2010.
Ellen Gibson	"Gory Cigarette Warnings Are Not New Around World," *Seattle Times*, June 21, 2011.
Dara Kam	"Lose Weight, Quit Smoking or Lose Medicaid Benefits?" *Palm Beach Post*, February 16, 2011.
Nathan Koppel	"Could New Cigarette Warning Labels Prompt Litigation?" *Wall Street Journal*, June 22, 2011.
Lyndsey Layton	"FDA Should Use Its Power to Lower Nicotine in Cigarettes, Former Chief Says," *Washington Post*, June 17, 2010.
Michael L. Marlow	"Do Smoking Bans Reduce Heart Attacks?" *Journal of American Physicians and Surgeons*, vol. 15, no. 1, Spring 2010, pp. 13–14.
A.G. Sulzberger	"Hospitals Shift Smoking Bans to Smoker Ban," *New York Times*, February 10, 2011.

OPPOSING
VIEWPOINTS®
SERIES

CHAPTER 3

Should Smoking
Alternatives Be
Regulated?

Chapter Preface

First invented by Chinese pharmacist Hon Lik in 2003, following the death of his father from lung cancer, the electronic cigarette, since popularly shortened to "e-cig," has in less than a decade become a hotter selling smoking replacement item than virtually any cessation product on the marketplace. Though intended more to resemble cigarettes packaged in attractive flavors like chocolate or strawberry than high-tech medical paraphernalia, e-cigs employ a miniature lithium battery that atomizes a liquid solution of nicotine released as vapor that looks like smoke but in chemical composition bears more in common with fog-machine fumes from a Hollywood movie set, accompanied by a small red light at the tip that blinks on with every drag.

Yet though simple in form and function, fewer products have been the subject of greater controversy among legislators or scientists with regard to its effectiveness as a quitting aid. Central to the dispute is the definition of what an e-cigarette actually is and who it is meant for. The FDA's original classification of electronic cigarettes as "drug delivery devices" was overturned in December 2010 by an appeals court in which the judges ruled that they could only be regulated as tobacco products and subsequently exempt from drug legislation. And despite Lik's initial conception and description of the devices as a "safer" nicotine substitute and their being heavily marketed as a "stop smoking" accessory, the crux of the manufacturers' winning defense in the trial was that electronic cigarettes are in fact designed for use by smokers regardless of whether they are trying to quit or cut down. Laws restricting or easing the import and sale of e-cigarettes vary wildly from region to region, with their use in public places banned in Washington State's King County while being allowed in bars and workplaces in adjacent Pierce County.

Conclusions drawn by researchers as to their safety and effectiveness have been equally mixed. Scientists who conducted one study at the University of California, Berkeley, concluded in the *Journal of Public Health Policy* that e-cigarettes demonstrated "tremendous promise in the fight against tobacco-related morbidity and mortality," while Dr. Edward Langston of the American Medical Association noted in 2010 that any product containing a toxic and addictive substance such as nicotine was impossible to endorse, and that their packaging "in fruit and candy flavors gives them the potential to entice new nicotine users, especially teens." In September 2008, the World Health Organization announced that it did not regard e-cigarettes as a legitimate aid to smoking cessation. Yet a Health New Zealand Ltd. study funded by major e-cigarette manufacturer Ruyan found that "[b]ased on the manufacturer's information, the composition of the cartridge liquid is not hazardous to health, if used as intended." And Elaine Keller, vice president of the Consumer Advocates for Smoke-Free Alternatives Association, claimed to be tobacco-free after forty-five years of smoking, purely as the result of her switching to e-cigarettes.

Just as the efficacy of nicotine patches or gum was once contested, debate over the potential benefits and risks of e-cigarettes is likely to continue for some time. The authors of the following viewpoints offer a wide range of views on which smoking alternatives justify further medical or legal consideration, as well as whether ultimately any method of nicotine intake is merely smoking repackaged.

| "Despite worldwide use, little is known about the properties of [electronic nicotine delivery systems], potential hazards or effects on health."

E-Cigarettes Are Dangerous and Need Better Regulation

Anna Trtchounian and Prue Talbot

Anna Trtchounian is a researcher at the University of California Riverside. Prue Talbot is a professor in the Department of Cell Biology and Neuroscience at the University of California Riverside. In the following viewpoint, researchers Trtchounian and Talbot offer the results of a study conducted on various brands of electronic cigarettes. According to their findings, the components of these alternative smoking devices lack important information regarding their content and use, as well as essential safety warnings. Additionally, they concluded that the cartridges leak nicotine, a dangerous and addictive chemical, and that there are no methods for proper disposal of the products or their accessories. Nicotine contamination from discarded cartridges, the authors note, could adversely affect the environment by entering water sources or soil. In conclusion, they advise that the manufacture, sales, quality control, and advertisement of such products should be subject to

Anna Trtchounian and Prue Talbot, "Electronic Nicotine Delivery Systems: Is There a Need for Regulation?," *Tobacco Control*, 2010, pp. 47–52. Copyright © 2010 by BMJ Publishing Group. All rights reserved. Reproduced by permission.

regulation at least as strict as that governing tobacco, although at the moment e-cigarettes are completely unregulated.

As you read, consider the following questions:
1. What information do the authors claim is missing from the labels of e-cigarette packaging and cartridges?
2. In what ways do the authors consider e-cigarettes to be environmentally unsafe?
3. In the authors' view, what regulatory steps regarding e-cigarettes should be undertaken?

Electronic nicotine delivery systems (ENDS) have gained worldwide usage with little information available on their health effects. Nicotine is an addictive and dangerous chemical that can cause death of adults at doses of 60 mg, promote tumour growth and be converted to carcinogens. In many US states, ENDS are readily available to anyone, including children, in shopping malls and on the internet. Despite worldwide use, little is known about the properties of ENDS, potential hazards or effects on health.

Investigations of the composition of ENDS aerosol have reached different conclusions. In an FDA report, the levels of carcinogens and diethylene glycol, a toxic contaminant, were sufficient to question safety and quality control, while a study supported by an ENDS manufacturer concluded that these products are safe. In a preliminary study involving humans, ENDS unexpectedly failed to elevate nicotine levels in the blood of smokers, calling into question their usefulness as nicotine delivery devices. The paucity of information on ENDS limits policymakers' ability to appraise the potential public health consequences of their widespread use. While some countries have banned ENDS, other countries, including the USA, are wrestling with regulation. More information about ENDS is needed to inform government decision-making.

We compared the design, labelling, packaging and accompanying print material for six brands of ENDS. Our data suggest that design improvements and regulation are needed to minimise potential hazards from ENDS.

Six brands of ENDS were evaluated. Cigarette kits and replacement cartridges were purchased from internet vendors. Design, nicotine content, labelling, leakiness, defective parts, disposal, errors in filling orders, instruction manual quality and advertising were evaluated for each brand. . . .

How E-Cigarettes Work

While all ENDS had a battery, atomiser and cartridge, design details of each brand differed. Battery length, cigarette colour and size of the air holes (not visible) near the red indicator light varied among brands. Manufacturers' names were printed on each battery, but it was sometimes difficult to distinguish between types of batteries within a brand. For example, the Crown Seven battery was not identified as the 'Hydro' model, and one Smoking Everywhere battery was not identified as the 'Platinum' model.

Atomisers had threads that screwed into the battery at one end and a U-shaped heating element that inserted into the cartridge at the opposite end. Atomisers from Liberty Stix, Crown Seven, Smoking Everywhere Gold and VapCigs were similar in design, but differed in length. Atomisers were not labelled, and some were interchangeable among brands. The Smoking Everywhere Platinum atomiser came embedded in the cartridge and was disposable.

Cartridges consisted of a reservoir that holds ENDS fluid and a mouthpiece. Reservoirs, varied in size, were open only at one end, and generally had flat surfaces that allowed aerosol to pass around the reservoir and into the mouthpiece. When assembled, the atomiser tip projected into the reservoir. Mouthpieces were generally cylindrical (NJOY was tapered), had a small air hole at one end and were wide open at the opposite end which slid into (NJOY) or over (all others) the atomiser.

To prevent fluid from escaping, cartridges had plastic plugs or caps at the large open end, except for VapCigs which had reservoirs sealed by aluminium foil. The open end of NJOY cartridges had a small rubber cap which was covered by a larger plastic cap. Prior to smoking, the plugs/caps were removed, and for VapCigs, the foil was punctured by the atomiser when the cigarette was assembled. Replacement cartridges came in plastic wrappers, except for Smoking Everywhere Platinum, which had only plastic caps on both ends.

Labels Without Information

All brands were sold with ambiguous amounts of nicotine/cartridge. Nicotine was usually indicted by a number followed by 'mg' (e.g., 24 mg). It was not clear if this was mg/cartridge or mg/ml. Values for nicotine ranged from 6 mg (NJOY) to 24 mg (Liberty Stix, Smoking Everywhere Platinum). Some cartridges claimed no nicotine (0 mg). Manufacturers used terms such as zero/no, low/light, medium, high and extra high to categorise nicotine strength. However, these terms usually referred to different nicotine concentrations when comparing across brands. For example, Liberty Stix high cartridges had 24 mg of nicotine, while Crown Seven Hydro high had 16 mg.

None of the cartridges was clearly labelled with the manufacturer's name, nicotine concentration, expiry date and flavour. Cartridges with no nicotine looked identical to those with high nicotine and were indistinguishable once removed from their wrappers or packs. Liberty Stix had the word 'Liberty' on a few cartridges. Smoking Everywhere Platinum had 16 mg or 24 mg stamped on cartridges with no indication of its meaning. The Liberty Stix, Crown Seven, Smoking Everywhere Gold and VapCigs cartridges looked similar and often could be interchanged among brands. The Smoking Everywhere Platinum starter kit was reported on its website and the starter kit case to come with high strength (16 mg) cartridges; however, the pack inside one kit was labelled '24 mg'.

Replacement cartridge wrappers were more informative than cartridges, although none clearly included the amount of nicotine and manufacturer's name. NJOY wrappers included strength (high, medium, low nicotine), flavour and expiry date. Smoking Everywhere Gold wrappers had flavour and a letter indicating strength, although labels were confusing (e.g., 'MIN Z' or 'TOB H' or 'Tobacco Original NO'). Crown Seven wrappers had strength (e.g., 'High') with no indication of flavour. Only Crown Seven's assorted pack wrappers indicated the specific flavour with strength. NJOY, Smoking Everywhere Gold and Crown Seven wrappers were labelled with small stickers that could easily fall off. Only a few Liberty Stix wrappers had the word 'Liberty' typed out, and none indicated strength or flavour. VapCigs starter kits included cartridges without wrappers, while replacement cartridge wrappers were unlabelled.

Replacement cartridges are sold in 'packs', which had labels with more information than cartridges and cartridge wrappers. However, packs in general were not uniformly labelled within or between brands.

Except for NJOY and Crown Seven, no packs indicated nicotine concentration, although all manufacturers attempted to indicate strength (e.g., high, medium, no nicotine) and flavour VapCigs packs had only strength (on all packs) and flavour (some packs) plus the letters 'VC' to indicate brand. Liberty Stix packs had flavour and strength with a handwritten dot next to a checkbox. Crown Seven indicated strength with a handwritten dot and flavour with either a handwritten dot or a small sticker. Terminology was inconsistent on Crown Seven's packs. For example, one pack had a handwritten dot next to 'espresso', while another had a 'coffee' sticker. It was not clear if these were the same flavours. Although there was a checkbox for the Crown Seven 'assorted' pack, 'assorted' was handwritten on packs. The pre-printed choices on the Crown Seven packs did not fully correspond to choices on their website, and none of the Crown Seven packs indicated the cartridges were for the Hydro model only. Smoking Everywhere packs were not uniform in their design, information or colour. Smoking Everywhere Gold packs did not state that cartridges were for the Gold kit only, while Platinum packs had 'Platinum' on four faces. The Gold tobacco flavoured packs had a sticker on the back side stating the flavour and strength as 'TOB H' or 'Tobacco Original NO', which were confusing. Mint flavoured packs had 'Mint' on the pack faces, yet used stickers on the back to indicate the flavour and strength, and again the code was cryptic (e.g., 'MIN H' or 'MIN L' or 'MIN Z'). NJOY had strength and flavour directly printed on packs.

Liberty Stix and Smoking Everywhere Platinum did not list cartridge ingredients. Smoking Everywhere Gold, Crown Seven and our original packs of NJOY listed ingredients as nicotine, water, flavouring (not specified) and propylene glycol. Recent shipments of NJOY included ethanol, glycerol, acetylpyrazine, guaiacol, mysomine, cotinine and vanillin. All packs listing ingredients included nicotine, even zero strength packs. All packs (including zero strength), except Crown Seven and VapCigs, had some form of warning regarding nicotine. Only some Smoking Everywhere Gold packs had a Surgeon General's warning. NJOY packs indicated the FDA had not approved the product, whereas Crown Seven and Liberty Stix packs had no FDA information. Some Smoking Everywhere packs mentioned the FDA, while others did not. Finally, some packs (NJOY and Smoking Everywhere Gold) indicated that the product was intended for adults and not pregnant women, but only NJOY, which had the most complete warning information, indicated possible side effects that may accompany use.

Defective Parts

Cartridges from most brands leaked nicotine-containing fluid from their reservoirs. When cartridges were removed from ENDS after smoking, beads of reservoir fluid were left adhering to the surface and heater tip of the atomiser and to the cartridges. Moreover, unused replacement cartridges (e.g., NJOY

An FDA Deputy Director Discusses Results of Testing E-Cigarettes

Results from these various tests raised two areas of concern: safety and product quality.

With respect to safety the majority of the samples tested positive for the presence of tobacco specific impurities suspected of being harmful to humans such as anabasine, myosmine, and beta-nicotyrine. These impurities have well defined specifications in the FDA approved smoking cessation products but not in these.

Half the samples also tested positive for the presence of certain tobacco specific nitrosoamines that are known human carcinogens such as N-(nitrosonornicotine), and 4-(methylnitrosoamino)-1-(3-pyridyl)-1-butanone. In addition to these carcinogenic impurities, one cartridge was found to have approximately 1% diethylene glycol present a toxic compound to humans. As far as the manufacturing quality some of the cartridges listed as containing no nicotine were actually found to have nicotine present.

Variability in the amount of nicotine delivered is also an issue. Three different cartridges with the same label contained significantly different amounts of nicotine per puff ranging anywhere from 27 to 43 micrograms. All of these results indicate a lack of general overall quality control.

Transcript from FDA's Media Briefing on Electronic Cigarettes, July 22, 2009.

and Liberty Stix) sometimes had beads of reservoir fluid on their surfaces and inside the sealed wrapper. It was difficult to load such cartridges onto an atomiser without getting reservoir fluid on our hands and other surfaces. When plugs were removed, reservoir fluid readily leaked out and if placed on a table, pools of reservoir fluid rapidly accumulated. NJOY instructions state 'Condensation and/or liquid may be seen inside the cellophane bag, which is a normal occurrence'. Smoking Everywhere Platinum, which had a disposable atomiser embedded in the reservoir, and VapCigs, which had a reservoir sealed by aluminium foil, presented the least potential for direct contact between the user's hands and reservoir fluid when assembling the cigarette. However, after use, even these better designs left reservoir fluid on the atomiser.

The NJOY kit arrived with dead batteries, which were quickly replaced. The red indicator tip at the end of the battery flashes a variable number of times if the battery is low or if the smoker is inhaling too many consecutive puffs. When ENDS were evaluated on a smoking machine, none of the flashing codes operated correctly all the time. Liberty Stix and VapCigs batteries were capable of lighting the red indicator light in the palm of our hands without the presence of an atomiser or cartridge. VapCigs released aerosol while held in our hands, apparently due to volatilisation of residual fluid on the surface of a new atomiser.

Cartridges stop producing aerosol after 100–200 puffs then need to be replaced by a fresh cartridge. Used cartridges contained liquid in their reservoirs (not shown). The amount of fluid left in spent cartridges was quite variable, with NJOY cartridges retaining the most fluid. None of the brands indicated a proper way to dispose of cartridges, wrappers, cartridge plugs, reservoirs, old batteries or old atomisers, and only NJOY and Crown Seven mentioned disposal at all in their instructions.

Most errors in filling internet orders involved sending cartridges with the wrong strength of nicotine (e.g., two of nine Crown Seven cartridges and two of 19 Liberty Stix cartridges were the wrong strength). Smoking Everywhere made numerous errors (e.g., repeatedly sent the wrong kits and cartridges), and even after 6 months, their orders were not completely filled correctly. NJOY filled all orders without error.

Instruction manuals were usually not complete and accurate. Instructions were specific for a brand, but not specific for the type of ENDS within a brand. For example, Smoking Everywhere's Platinum instructions included information for a different model (their 'Mini Electronic Cigarette'). We evaluated the instruction manuals using a 100-point questionnaire (25 yes/no questions each worth four points). Based on this questionnaire, NJOY had the best manual and VapCigs had the least helpful.

Truth in Advertisement

On both websites and in print material, we found numerous statements regarding ENDS that were not based on scientific findings and for which there is no rigorous supporting data. Examples of such statements include: 'Be careful to avoid inhaling any significant quantity of liquid. Although it gives you a slight tingling sensation, it is not harmful' (Liberty Stix); 'Within 2 weeks, your lung capacity will increase by 30%. Your energy levels will increase. Your throat and lungs will feel markedly better! Wrinkles in your skin will become less noticeable and colour will return to your skin' (Liberty Stix). One pack (Smoking Everywhere) was labelled 'Vitamin', although no indication of what this meant was given.

Our data show that ENDS labelling, design features, print material and disposal need improvement. Labelling of ENDS cartridges and wrappers was generally poor. Direct clear labelling of cartridges, wrappers and packs with accurate nicotine concentrations is needed to minimise inadvertent exposure to nicotine and is particularly important given the high number of errors made in filling orders with cartridges of incorrect strength. Non-smokers could easily mistake 24-mg cartridges for 0-mg cartridges and in the process become addicted to nicotine. Likewise former smokers could become re-addicted by inadvertently smoking nicotine-containing cartridges. Full warnings regarding nicotine (it can be deadly, addictive and converted to carcinogens) should appear on all packs, and instruction manuals should provide complete accurate information on the product.

It was difficult to avoid touching nicotine-containing reservoir fluid when handling cartridges, which presents health risks to ENDS users and non-users. Nicotine can be absorbed though the skin and cause harm, especially if amounts are large. Nicotine deposited on surfaces (skin, table, counters) can be converted into carcinogens, as shown with third-hand smoke. This point raises serious health issues relating to nicotine leakage from cartridges during and after use. What are the consequences of long-term handling of nicotine and conversion of nicotine into carcinogens on the skin or in the environment of ENDS users? These questions should be answered before use of ENDS is allowed.

Used cartridges contained fluid after they ceased producing aerosol. Regulatory agencies need to address how to safely dispose of used cartridges and minimise introduction of nicotine into the environment. Studies documenting hazards associated with disposal of cigarette butts led to regulation of butt disposal in Australia, where fines are issued to those who do not deposit butts in valid receptacles. Residual nicotine in spent ENDS cartridges can leak onto surfaces where conversion to carcinogens could take place. Furthermore, as nicotine from used ENDS cartridges leaches into water supplies, it may directly affect aquatic life and could be propagated through the food chain. Proper disposal of ENDS cartridges should be addressed before spent cartridges present a serious health problem.

Better regulation of ENDS sales and distribution is needed to protect children and adults from nicotine exposure and possible addiction. Our observations provide evidence that regulators should consider removing ENDS from the market until design features, quality control, labelling, disposal and safety issues have been adequately addressed.

"*There appears to be a very strong bias operating which does not allow anti-smoking researchers to objectively view the scientific evidence on electronic cigarettes.*"

E-Cigarette Vapor Is Less Harmful than Secondhand Smoke

Michael Siegel

Michael Siegel is a professor in the Department of Community Health Sciences at Boston University School of Public Health. He has published nearly seventy papers on the topic of tobacco. In the following viewpoint, Siegel takes issue with a report in the journal Annals of Internal Medicine *in which the authors urge physicians to advise their patients not to use electronic cigarettes as a method of quitting smoking. Siegel notes that the report is riddled with what he claims are gross inaccuracies, the most egregious of which is the authors' claim that there is no evidence suggesting that e-cigarette vapor is safer than exposure to regular secondhand smoke. Siegel argues that making such unsubstantiated statements is not only fallacious but dangerous, because they will lead smokers to mistakenly conclude that the reverse is also true: Secondhand smoke is no more dangerous than e-cigarette fumes. Furthermore, such false equivalencies could also be interpreted by smokers as an excuse to maintain their regular smoking habits rather than use e-cigarettes, a far less dangerous alternative in Siegel's view, as a substitute.*

As you read, consider the following questions:

1. According to the author, what false conclusion was reached regarding the relative safety of electronic cigarettes?
2. What scientific evidence involving carcinogen levels in e-cigarettes does the author maintain is being "irrationally" disregarded by antismoking researchers?
3. What bias does the author accuse antismoking researchers of harboring with regard to e-cigarettes?

In an interview published by the journal *Annals of Internal Medicine*, one of the co-authors of a commentary urging physicians to counsel their patients against the use of electronic cigarettes as a tool for smoking cessation tells the public that there is no evidence that electronic cigarette vapor is any safer than exposure to secondhand smoke from regular cigarettes.

The researcher also tells the public that there is no evidence that the use of electronic cigarettes is any safer than cigarette smoking.

After noting that some electronic cigarette companies are using marketing terms which suggest that their products are safer than cigarettes to both users and non-users, the researcher states: "There isn't empirical data to suggest that that's true."

Of course, what the researcher is therefore telling the public is that there is no evidence that smoking is any more hazardous than inhaling the trace levels of carcinogens in electronic cigarettes.

How Safe Are E-Cigarettes?

"The other products are only replacing nicotine; this product is also dealing with the behavioral aspect of smoking," says Michael Siegel, MD, the associate chairman of community health sciences at the Boston University School of Public Health. . . .

"Holding and puffing are all part of addiction," he explains.

They are not risk-free, he says—just less risky than cigarettes.

Denise Mann, "E-Cigarettes: Safe Enough to Help You Quit?" health.com, February 26, 2010.

He is also telling the public that there is no evidence that secondhand smoke exposure is any more hazardous than exposure to the vapor from electronic cigarette use.

I have already argued that the advice to physicians to counsel their smoking patients not to quit smoking using electronic cigarettes is irresponsible and misguided. In instructing patients or smokers in general not to use electronic cigarettes, what these researchers are saying is that they would rather smokers continue to smoke cigarettes than to quit smoking via the help of electronic cigarettes.

The reality is that the majority of smokers are not going to be able to quit smoking using traditional therapy (i.e., pharmaceutical aids). For this overwhelming majority of smokers, the study authors are saying: "Don't try electronic cigarettes. We don't know what they are. Stick with the real ones. Don't put down your Marlboros, Camels, and Newports."

Flawed Research

Now, the story expands. Not only are these researchers providing misguided and irresponsible advice, but they are now misleading the public by suggesting that there is no evidence that smoking is any more harmful than vaping or that secondhand smoke is any more dangerous than exposure to exhaled electronic cigarette vapor.

These are dangerous and misleading statements. They imply that smoking is not all that hazardous, since if it is no worse than electronic cigarette use, it involves only exposure to minute levels of carcinogens (as has been documented to be the case with electronic cigarettes). And it implies that secondhand smoke exposure is not hazardous at all, since there is no evidence whatsoever that being in the presence of an e-cigarette user is harmful.

The researcher acknowledges that only trace levels of carcinogens were found in electronic cigarettes. He also acknowledges that the propylene glycol used in electronic cigarettes is not worrisome. How, then, can he go on to state that there is no evidence that electronic cigarettes are any safer than what we already know is the most dangerous and toxic consumer product on the market, which we know kills hundreds of thousands of Americans each year?

It is even less rational to suggest that secondhand smoke exposure is no worse than exposure to the greatly diluted, exhaled vapor from e-cigarette users. We know that the quantities of carcinogens delivered to the nonuser are miniscule.

It doesn't take a rocket toxicologist to figure out that the current data on the levels of carcinogens in cigarettes versus electronic cigarettes does provide strong evidence that vaping is less hazardous than smoking, and that exposure to the vapor exhaled by e-cigarette users is less hazardous than exposure to secondhand smoke.

In fact, I have estimated that the level of tobacco-specific nitrosamines in electronic cigarettes is about 1,400 times lower than that in Marlboros. In light of these data, how can one possibly argue that there is no evidence that smoking Marlboros is any more dangerous than using an electronic cigarette?

A Dangerous Bias

It is problematic enough to disseminate irresponsible advice to the public about such an important health issue as quitting smoking. But to base that advice on blatant misrepresentations of the available scientific data to the public is even worse.

Why are these researchers ignoring the available data which clearly show that the levels of carcinogens in electronic cigarettes are orders of magnitude lower than in regular cigarettes?

Unfortunately, there appears to be a very strong bias operating which does not allow anti-smoking researchers to objectively view the scientific evidence on electronic cigarettes. I believe that the very fact that these devices are similar to cigarettes blinds many anti-smoking researchers to the actual scientific evidence that is readily available. It is apparently not the documented hazards of vaping which are troubling the anti-smoking movement, but the fact that it looks like smoking.

How can anything which looks like smoking be a good thing, even if there is strong evidence that these products are bringing immense and immediate health benefits to thousands of users?

| *"Flavored cigarettes attract and allure kids into addiction."*

Banning Flavored Cigarettes Prevents Addiction by Young People

Kathleen Quinn, Lawrence Deyton, Howard Koh, and Margaret Hamburg

Kathleen Quinn is a spokesperson at the Center for Tobacco Products. Lawrence Deyton is the center's operating director. Howard Koh is the assistant secretary for health at the Department of Health and Human Services. Margaret Hamburg is the commissioner of the Food and Drug Administration. The following viewpoint is taken from a transcript of a media briefing held by the newly formed government agency the Center for Tobacco Products on the subject of banning "cigarettes with certain characterizing flavors" as part of the Family Smoking Prevention and Tobacco Control Act signed into law by President Barack Obama on June 22, 2009. Here they assert that banning clove cigarettes is a moral imperative of substantial urgency intended to prevent dangerously addictive products marketed to youths from being readily available.

As you read, consider the following questions:

1. On what grounds do Howard Koh and Margaret Hamburg claim that banning clove cigarettes is "crucial" to "protecting [the] nation's health"?

2. In what four ways does Lawrence Deyton claim the agency is intending to support the ban?

3. What is one of the uncertain aspects of the ban raised by one of the journalists?

Excerpts from the Transcript for FDA [Food and Drug Administration]'s Media Briefing on Ban on Cigarettes with Certain Characterizing Flavors
   Moderator: Kathleen Quinn
   September 22, 2009
   9:30 AM CT

Kathleen Quinn: Hello everybody. I'm Kathleen Quinn with the Center for Tobacco Products. I'd like to start off by thanking you all for joining us today regarding the ban on cigarettes with certain characterizing flavors.

We're going to start today's call with some opening remarks. I have with me today Dr. Howard Koh, the Assistant Secretary for Health at the Department of Health and Human Services, Dr. Margaret Hamburg, Commissioner of Food and Drugs, and Dr. Lawrence Deyton, our new director for the Center for Tobacco Products.

In the room we also have some technical experts who we may turn to on certain topics. If in fact they do need to answer a question, we will identify them by name and title. And with that I'd like to turn it over to Dr. Koh.

Howard Koh: Thank you very much, Miss Quinn, and good morning everyone and thank you everyone for joining us on this very important call. . . .

The FDA has just established a Center for Tobacco Products as part of a historic new effort to curb the hundreds of thousands of preventable deaths caused by tobacco products each year.

As you will hear, this Center will be overseeing the implementation of the Family Smoking Prevention and Tobacco Control Act, which was signed into law by President [Barack] Obama on June 22, 2009. To protect public health, this historic act gives the FDA new authority to regulate marketing and promotion of tobacco products. We are here today because we know that tobacco addiction is a public health catastrophe.

According to the Centers for Disease Control and Prevention, cigarette smoking causes an estimated 438,000 deaths, or about one in every five deaths each year in this country, and on average adults who smoke cigarettes die 14 years earlier than nonsmokers. So it's clear that regulating tobacco is critical to saving lives. . . .

Today the FDA is announcing a ban on cigarettes with characterizing fruit, candy, and clove flavors—cigarettes that have special appeal for children. Flavored cigarettes attract and allure kids into addiction. And so the agency's national effort to enforce this provision of a new act and to advise parents about the dangers of flavored tobacco products is an important first step for responsible tobacco regulation that will protect the American public. Now I am very pleased and honored to turn this call over to Dr. Hamburg.

Margaret Hamburg: Thank you, Howard. It's really a pleasure to work with you on such an important health issue, and of course with all of the other members of our team working on our tobacco efforts. Before we get into the specifics of today's action, I'd like to start by providing the media with a bit of a progress update on the larger implementation of the act.

FDA has taken many important steps in just a few short months since enactment of the Family Smoking Prevention and Tobacco Control Act on June 22, 2009.

We've officially established the Center for Tobacco Products, hired a center director, Dr. Lawrence Deyton, who's here with us today, created the Tobacco Products Scientific Advisory Committee, opened a public docket to receive input on implementation of the act, conducted listening sessions with many stakeholder groups, and established relationships with our state and local partners.

As Dr. Koh stated, almost 90% of adult smokers start smoking as teenagers, and these flavored cigarettes are a gateway for many children and young adults to become regular smokers. As a physician, a public health official, and a parent, I know just how important today's action is in taking another step toward protecting the health of America's children and ultimately reducing the burden of illness and death caused by tobacco use.

With me today is another physician who also knows just how crucial today's ban is to protecting our nation's health. . . . Dr. Lawrence Deyton, our new center director. Many of you may recognize Dr. Deyton's name from his long public health career, but I am so excited to be able to introduce him to you all today as FDA's first director for the Center for Tobacco Products. . . .

Lawrence Deyton: Thank you very much, Dr. Hamburg, for your gracious introduction, and I want to thank all of you on the phone for participating in this call today. This will be the first of what will no doubt be many opportunities for us to talk about FDA's implementation of the Family Smoking Prevention and Tobacco Control Act signed by President Obama just three months ago today.

The goal[s] of this law include reducing tobacco use in youth, reducing the toll of tobacco-related diseases [and] disability . . . , and promoting public understanding of the content and consequences of the use of tobacco products.

Effective today there is a ban on cigarettes with certain characterizing fruit, candy, herb, and spice flavors. The reason for this is such an important step, clear and simple. It is to protect our children from initiating tobacco use.

Each day in the United States approximately 3,600 young people between the ages of 12 and 17 initiate cigarette smoking, and an estimated 1,100 young people become daily cigarette smokers. Flavors make cigarettes and other tobacco products more appealing to youth. Studies show that 17-year-old smokers are three times as likely to use flavored cigarettes as smokers over the age of 25.

The appeal of flavored tobacco to youth is well known to the tobacco industry as well. For example an historic memo from one manufacturer instructed workers to, "Make a cigarette which is obviously youth-oriented. This could involve cigarette name, blend, flavor, and marketing technique. For example, a flavor which would be candy-like but give the satisfaction of a cigarette."

Advisors to another company developed concepts for youth cigarettes, including cola and apple flavors, and a sweet flavored cigarette saying, "It's a well-known fact that teenagers like sweet products. Honey might be considered."

Candy and fruit flavored cigarettes are a gateway for many children and young adults to become regular tobacco users. That is why the Family Smoking Prevention and Tobacco Control Act specifically bans these products. As of today, manufacturers should no longer make, distributors should no longer distribute, importers should no longer import, and retailers should no longer sell these products.

Here is what the agency is doing to support this law. First, even though the ban on flavored cigarettes is a well-known part of the Family Smoking Prevention and Tobacco Control Act, FDA notified the tobacco industry, distributors, and retailers last week of our intent to enforce this ban on the earliest date authorized to do so, and that is today.

Second, FDA has established a toll-free number at 1-877-CTP -1373, and a website for the public at www.FDA.gov/flavoredto

bacco—one word—for reporting violations. Today we are publishing a notice in the Federal Register with this information.

Third, we've notified our sister federal agencies, as well as state and local tobacco control officials around the country, so that they can educate their constituencies about the ban on flavored cigarettes and how to report violations via phone, website, or the mail.

Fourth, we've established procedures at the border to watch for products which violate this ban to prevent them from entering the United States. And fifth, we've created a team to review the reports that [it] receives, and oversee appropriate action by the agency. Members of this team will be meeting daily starting tomorrow.

FDA is also releasing and distributing widely a press release, also in Spanish, a parental advisory, and a fact sheet about flavored tobacco products. These documents are especially important for parents, family members, doctors and the—and health providers, school teachers, church youth group leaders, and anyone who cares for children and young adults. This advisory is designed to make sure we all have the facts about the dangers of all types of flavored tobacco products.

Thank you for the opportunity to speak with you today on this very important public health step. The tobacco team and I look forward to your questions. Thanks very much.

Kathleen Quinn: (Melissa), this is Kathleen. We are ready to open up the line for questions. We would like to get questioners' names and affiliations, and we'd also like to take one question and one follow up.

Questions from the Media

Coordinator: Yes ma'am. Thank you. . . . The first question comes from Gardner Harris, the *New York Times*. Your line is open.

Gardner Harris: Hi. You all have banned flavorings in cigarettes. Have you made any decisions about what to do about flavorings in other forms of tobacco—small cigars, smokeless tobacco, snuff, other things like that? Thanks.

Lawrence Deyton: This is Dr. Deyton. I'll start the answer. The act provides us with authority today to ban cigarettes with certain characterizing flavors. Other flavored tobacco products are issues which we will be studying and certainly be discussing with the Scientific Advisory Committee, which is being set up.

Coordinator: Thank you. The next is from Jennifer Corbett, *Wall Street Journal*. Your line is open.

Jennifer Corbett: Yes, hi. I think this is just a follow to Gardner's question. The question I have is—and you mentioned in your press release—that you're looking at menthol cigarettes, because my understanding (about) is the—that's the biggest flavor out there that . . .

Lawrence Deyton: Yes, the menthol issue is also specifically addressed in the Family Smoking Prevention and Tobacco Control Act, and that is an issue again which we will be discussing with our Scientific Advisory Committee and studying. We've been asked specifically by the act to study that.

I think it's important to emphasize that—and I do refer all of you to the FDA advisory, which we're posting on our website today—that is specific[ally] targeted to parents and family members and anyone interested in flavored tobacco products. That's information that I think any parent—any of us wants to know and be able to communicate to our children and youth about these products.

Kathleen Quinn: Thank you. Next question?

Coordinator: The next question is from Jim Carroll, the *Louisville Courier-Journal*. Your line's open.

Jim Carroll: Oh, hi. Dr. Deyton, question about enforcement here. Are you saying basically that it's up to the consumers to sort of report this via website, mail, phone calls, things like that? The FDA doesn't really have the troops obviously at this point to do this, right?

Lawrence Deyton: We—FDA certainly has enforcement and compliance staff that are enforcing this ban today. So the full power and resources of the FDA are on this right now.

Jim Carroll: But I—in terms of you don't have inspectors going around checking retail stores across the United States, do you? Or maybe you do. I mean who would be doing this?

Lawrence Deyton: Let me introduce Catherine Lorraine, who's a lawyer with our staff. Catherine?

Catherine Lorraine: I think as Dr. Deyton said, we do have the full resources of the agency behind us. I think we will be working with our enforcement team to find the most effective ways of identifying violations of this act, and we will be bringing appropriate enforcement actions when we do document violations.

Lawrence Deyton: To the first part of your question, though, there certainly is—we are encouraging consumers, parents, the public, to let us know through those numbers and by mail and on the website of a possible violation. So the public really is our partner in this activity very much. . . .

Coordinator: The next question is from (Dan Schiff, *Tan Sheet*). Your line's open.

Dan Schiff: Yes, thanks very much for taking my question. I was just wondering if this ban extends to the smokeless electronic cigarettes that have become popular. And if not, is that something you're looking at and planning to act on soon?

Lawrence Deyton: I think that the answer to that question is that we're—there's a lawsuit around that right now. And I don't think that we are allowed to talk about that. Catherine, did you want to [say] anything else about that?

Catherine Lorraine: No, we don't comment on lawsuits in litigation. . . .

Coordinator: The next question is from Daniel DeNoon from WebMD. Your line is open.

Daniel DeNoon: Thank you for taking my question. I'm still a little confused about exactly what is banned. It's my understanding that we're talking about any product that's wrapped in paper and contains tobacco. Does this mean that cigars—small cigars that are—that may be wrapped in tobacco leaf and contain flavored tobacco are not included in the ban?

And does the ban—I know that you can't talk about the eCigarette regulation, but can I assume that that means that eCigarettes are not at this time included in this specific ban? Thank you.

Lawrence Deyton: The definition of a cigarette is that it has these characterizing flavors is what is banned. So it's not what is labeled, it's what is the actual product and its intended use.

Daniel DeNoon: So if it's wrapped in a tobacco leaf does that make it not covered in the ban?

Lawrence Deyton: The—if it—according to the law, as (my reading the) law—and I'm not a lawyer—but if something is wrapped in a tobacco leaf, and is—would not be considered a—hold on just a second.

Catherine Lorraine: We'd like—this is Catherine Lorraine in the Center. I just want to draw your attention to the portion of the definition of a cigarette, which specifically refers to the appearance of the product and how it is perceived and offered for sale to consumers. And so we will be looking at products on an individual basis to determine if it meets that aspect of the definition of a cigarette.

Coordinator: Thank you. The next question is from Miriam Falco from CNN. Your line is open.

Miriam Falco: Hi, it's Miriam Falco. Thanks for taking the question. I got to say I'm a little confused. Your answers are all very government-speak, if I may say so. If you know that young people prefer menthol cigarettes, then why aren't they included in this? And how many cigarettes are we talking about that are flavored? I mean what numbers are we talking about? And since you notified the industry last week, what's their response been?

Lawrence Deyton: In terms of the question of menthol, the law specifically asks us to look at menthol separately. And we will be doing that. And I'm not aware of response from industry. We certainly have had—we had listening sessions with industry on this end—the implementation of the act itself—and, you know, frankly I was impressed. You know, industry are taking this very seriously and recognize that—and are responding.

Kathleen Quinn: Miriam, do you have a follow-up?

Miriam Falco: Well, yes. How many—I mean you mentioned the statistics on how, you know, [a] 17 year old is three times more likely to try a flavored cigarette. But I mean can you give me some kind of numbers as to how many cigarettes are consumed by young people—a frame of reference?

Lawrence Deyton: I don't think anyone around this table has that number. We can get—yes, we can get back to you with that.

Kathleen Quinn: Thanks, Miriam. Next question.

Coordinator: The next question is from Brian Hartman, ABC News.

Brian Hartman: Yes, hi. Could you sort of lay out some of the next steps that you're going to be taking? What are the next big sort of restrictions that the law has put in your lap?

Lawrence Deyton: The next big step is to ask and instruct the industry for registering with us. The law asked us—requires us to have the tobacco industry registered with the FDA, and then we also will be requesting from them the specific constituents and components of tobacco products be reported to the FDA. So that is the next big step.

What that will allow us to do is work with industry to understand what are the components of tobacco products so that we can again look at the protection of public health—reducing youth smoking, reduce the toll of diseases related to tobacco use, and very importantly promote understanding of the contents and consequences of [the] use of tobacco products.

Brian Hartman: Marketing and labeling—are those steps that you also have to take soon?

Lawrence Deyton: That is certainly of—as the dominos fall in the regulatory requirements, the law allows us to get into those issues. The reinstatement of the 1996 regulation about those issues

Marketing Flavored Tobacco Products

In recent years, tobacco manufacturers have introduced and marketed fruit, alcohol and even candy-flavored cigarettes, cigars, smokeless tobacco products and less conventional tobacco products. From strawberry to exotic midnight berry, the new flavors are unlike anything marketed in the United States in the past. Some of the new flavors include cherry, blueberry, peach, grape, pineapple, watermelon, toffee, chocolate, chocolate mint, vanilla, rum, pina colada and margarita.

These flavorings form the basis of marketing campaigns. For example, Apple Blend Skoal Chew is said to "combine rich, premium tobacco with the crisp flavor of juicy apples" while the marketing of Kool Smooth Fusions Caribbean Chill Cigarettes promises a "splash of citrus flavor to offer a uniquely refreshing taste." One of Dean's Little Cigars touts "a nice punch of 'wild raspberry' to tantalize the taste buds." The advertisements and packaging employ stylish designs and bright colors that further emphasize the flavor. In fact, nearly every aspect of the marketing for these flavored tobacco products, except the health warnings, is strikingly similar to the marketing used for similarly flavored candies and sweetened beverages.

Kathleen Dachille, Pick Your Poison:
Responses to Marketing and Sale of Flavored
Tobacco Products, *Tobacco Control Legal
Consortium, 2009.*

is on the menu of the issues that we'll be dealing with very soon as well.

Kathleen Quinn: (Melissa), I believe we're ready for our last question.

Coordinator: Yes ma'am. The last question comes from Lyndsey Layton, *Washington Post*.

Lyndsey Layton: Hi. Thanks very much. Dr. Deyton I just wanted to ask that given the fact that a lot of these products—the flavored cigarettes—are coming from overseas and much has been made of the Agency's challenge in, you know, at the border manpower shortage, I'm just wondering—when you said that procedures at the border have been in place or new procedures now, can you elaborate on that a little bit? What do you mean by that? Are there actually additional bodies at the border, or what are you doing to control the import?

Lawrence Deyton: We have sent specific instructions to the enforcement team that works the border issues about this to define and discuss exactly what this ban is, and they are doing that.

Lyndsey Layton: So you're working then with the existing staff that you have at the borders. It's not like you've put additional bodies in place.

Lawrence Deyton: The answer—yes, the—we have—we—it's existing staff that is in place now.

Kathleen Quinn: Okay, thank you all so much for joining us today. The replay of this call should be available shortly, and we will post a transcript of it on our website. . . .

Coordinator: This does conclude today's conference. You may now disconnect.

> "The Indonesian government . . . claims
> 'no scientific evidence . . . has been
> produced to show the specific health
> risks of clove cigarette[s] that would
> warrant banning this cigarette, but not
> menthol.'"

Banning Flavored Cigarettes Is Protectionism Disguised as Public Service

Elizabeth Nolan Brown

Elizabeth Nolan Brown is a professional journalist, essayist, and blogger. In the following viewpoint, she maintains that the Food and Drug Administration (FDA)'s ban of flavored cigarettes has nothing to do with "protecting children" as the legislators assert but everything to do with shutting down the import of flavored cigarettes that compete with American-made menthol cigarettes, which, as even the FDA admits, are far more popular with youths than cloves or other flavored cigarettes. Brown notes that there appears to be little consistency from the ban's sponsors as to why menthols should be exempt save those involving profits.

As you read, consider the following questions:

1. What discrepancy does the author find the FDA and US Senate are culpable of with regard to legislation banning cloves and not menthols?

2. What two conflicting reasons does press secretary Melissa Wagoner offer as to why menthols are exempted from the ban and in what ways does the author find her responses "Orwellian"?

3. Outside of the trade controversy, what is one reason stated in the viewpoint that the author claims is a good one for opposing a ban on clove cigarettes?

The clove cigarette has become something of a cliche. With its dark wrapper and strong, peculiar—and, to many, sickening—smell, it's best known as the prop de rigueur [proscribed by custom] of sullen, artistic-leaning college kids and people who read too many vampire novels. Recently, however, it has taken on a new role: center of an international trade feud.

Legislation in the U.S. Senate would ban cloves, along with several other flavored cigarette varieties, under the mantra so oft-used to ban things these days: protecting the children. The measure—part of a broader tobacco regulation bill granting the Food and Drug Administration the power to regulate tobacco products—has ignited controversy with the government of Indonesia, which claims the proposed ban represents a "serious trade issue" and has threatened to file a formal challenge with the World Trade Organization should the bill become law.

"If the legislation has the effect of only or primarily banning Indonesian cigarettes ... then there could be a case that the bill is targeted at Indonesia," says Daniel Ikenson, associate director of the Center for Trade Policy Studies at the Cato Institute.

Made from a mix of tobacco and clove leaves, clove cigarettes —or *kreteks*, as they are known in Indonesia—are a major Indonesian export to the United States. In 2006, Indonesia made more than 99 percent of the clove cigarettes imported by the U.S., to the tune of $10.28 million. Indonesia is home to more than 500 *kretek* manufacturers (including leading brands Sampoerna and Djarum), and the *kretek* industry is the country's largest employer.

The Indonesian government called the proposed ban "discriminatory and protectionist," claiming *kreteks* are more similar to menthol cigarettes, which are specifically exempted from the ban, than to other flavored varieties. It claims "no scientific evidence . . . has been produced to show the specific health risks of clove cigarette[s] that would warrant banning this cigarette, but not menthol." Unlike clove cigarettes, however, most menthol cigarettes are manufactured in the U.S.

Disguised Protectionism?

This apparent discrepancy in treatment of foreign and domestic cigarettes has left legislators scrambling to refute Indonesia's not-entirely-unreasonable charges of "disguised protectionism."

Melissa Wagoner, press secretary for Sen. Ted Kennedy, D-Mass. (who introduced the measure in the Senate), offers a strangely Orwellian [a policy of control by propaganda] rationalization: banning menthol smoking will actually *harm* menthol smokers!

"Menthol cigarettes have been on the market for decades and a substantial number of smokers have developed a dependency on them," says Wagoner. Were menthols banned, these smokers might turn to "illicit, black market tobacco products that are even more dangerous to their health," she explains.

Meanwhile, Sen. Mike Enzi (R-WY) insists the discrepancy is protectionism—for the ever-villainous "Big Tobacco," which dares suggest it's in business to make a profit and should therefore sell whatever products (legal, adult) consumers like best.

But "unscrupulous tobacco companies" use "flavors like clove" to lure teenagers into smoking, says Senator Enzi, who is, at least, consistent: this putative small-government conservative champions banning both cloves and menthols.

Selective Sales Ban?

The sales ban [of flavored cigarettes] is supposed to keep kids from being lured into the world of nicotine addiction by fruit, candy and chocolate flavors.

Statistically, however, the flavor kids consider tastiest is straight-up tobacco, in the form of Marlboro brand cigarettes (produced by Philip Morris). Some 81 percent of established teen smokers consider Marlboro to be their ticket to flavor country, according to a February 12 [2009] article.

The next most popular flavor is mint.

Sarah Torribio, "Flavor Cigarette Ban Curbs Freedom, Helps Big Tobacco Keep Selling," L.A. Health and Beauty Examiner, August 23, 2009, Examiner.com.

Minority Report

Senator Enzi should check the data about teen clove smoking, though: According to the U.S. Centers for Disease Control, clove cigarettes make up only a small percentage of teen and tween tobacco use. The 2004 National Youth Tobacco Survey found that among high school students, cloves accounted for only 2.3 percent of tobacco use, with regular cigarettes accounting for 22.3 percent, followed by cigars (12.8 percent), smokeless tobacco (6.0 percent), pipes (3 percent) and bidis (2.6 percent). Among middle school students, cloves made up just 1.5 percent of tobacco use (in comparison with 8.1 percent for regular cigarettes and 5.2 percent for cigars).

The Specialty Tobacco Council points out that cloves generally cost more than regular cigarettes and are typically sold only in high-end tobacco shops, making them less attractive and available to minors. If legislators are really in this to protect the children, a ban on menthols—which are more easily accessible, possibly harder to quit, and which several studies have shown to be popular among teens (especially low-income African American teens)—would at least make more sense.

But "unlike other flavorings, menthol cigarettes constitute a major share—about 27 percent—of the [US] market," says Wagoner, a statement laughably antithetical to her assertions that ban decisions are based solely on health-and-welfare of smokers rationale.

"It seems . . . this [is] feel-good, do-nothing legislation that's typical of Congress these days," says David Harsanyi, *Denver Post* columnist and author of *Nanny State*.

Unsurprisingly, the measure has "strong bipartisan support," according to Wagoner. "It is widely expected to be enacted in this Congress."

A spokesman from the Embassy of Indonesia's Office of Agriculture said his country would back off its trade complaint should the ban be changed to include menthol cigarettes.

Even if the trade issue can be overcome, however, Harsanyi notes another reason to oppose a ban on clove cigarettes: "Smoking is a legal activity, and American adults should be able to make the choice about which flavors they smoke."

It sounds entirely too sensible, doesn't it? Really—won't Harsanyi please think of the liberal arts students and Ann Rice-fans?

| "Smokeless tobacco products are not
safer alternatives to cigarette smoking."

Smokeless Tobacco Is Just as Harmful as Cigarettes

Lorinda Bullock

Lorinda Bullock is associate editor of the Elsevier Global Medical News. In the following viewpoint, she describes findings by the American Heart Association verifying that, contrary to articles from other sources, smokeless tobacco products are not superior alternatives to cigarettes, do not help smokers quit, and when used long-term increase the risk of heart attacks, strokes, and cancer. Bullock notes that while chewing tobacco use has been on the decline in the United States since the 1980s, snuff is gaining popularity, especially in youth brackets.

As you read, consider the following questions:

1. According to the article, what types of nicotine replacement therapy, if any, does the American Heart Association endorse and what makes these types different from smokeless tobacco?

2. What do the researchers quoted in the article claim makes smokeless tobacco hazardous?

3. What social or psychological factors might account for the statistic cited in the article that smokeless tobacco use is more prevalent among young men than any other demographic?

Smokeless tobacco products are not safer alternatives to cigarette smoking, they do not help smokers quit, and their long-term use can, in fact, increase the risk of fatal heart attack, fatal stroke, and cancer, the American Heart Association [AHA] warned in a scientific statement.

The researchers, led by Mariann R. Piano, Ph.D., examined several international studies to compare smokeless tobacco use and its health risks.

Meta-analysis data involving male, Swedish smokers [from] 1976–2002 showed a significant decrease in cigarette smoking that corresponded with an increase in use of smokeless tobacco products, the investigators wrote in the AHA journal, *Circulation*. Despite the decline in cigarette use, concern is warranted, Dr. Piano, professor of biobehavioral science at the University of Illinois at Chicago, explained: "Smokeless tobacco products are harmful and addictive—that does not translate to a better alternative," Dr. Piano said in a written statement released by the association.

"Scientists and policy makers need to assess the effect of 'reduced risk' messages related to smokeless tobacco use on public perception, especially among smokers who might be trying to quit," Dr. Piano and her colleagues wrote.

Citing "inadequate evidence of smoking cessation efficacy and safety," the researchers deemed as inappropriate the promotion of smokeless tobacco as a way to reduce smoking-related diseases.

The American Heart Association does recommend nicotine replacement therapy (nicotine gum or a nicotine-releasing patch placed on the skin) as a safer option for cigarette smokers wanting to quit. "Clinical studies have found no increased risk

What Are the Ingredients in Smokeless Tobacco?

- Polonium 210 (nuclear waste)
- N-Nitrosamines (cancer-causing)
- Formaldehyde (embalming fluid)
- Nicotine (addictive drug)
- Cadmium (used in batteries and nuclear reactor shields)
- Cyanide (poisonous compound)
- Arsenic (poisonous metallic element)
- Benzene (used in insecticide and motor fuel)
- Lead (nerve poison)

American Academy of Otolaryngology,
"Smokeless Tobacco—Insight into Its Effects on
the Body," December 2010, entnet.org.

of heart attack or stroke with either type of nicotine replacement therapy," the AHA said in the written statement.

Meta-analysis data in the association's scientific statement http://circ.ahajournals.org/cgi/reprint/CIR.0b013e3181f432c3 indicated that smokeless tobacco use was associated with an increased risk of heart disease.

Additionally, a sub-analysis of INTERHEART (a study of 15,152 cases of first myocardial infarction in 52 countries) showed that tobacco chewers had a significantly increased risk of first myocardial infarction compared with those who never used tobacco. Two other meta-analyses indicated that smokeless tobacco use was also associated with an increased risk of fatal stroke.

The researchers explained that, like cigarettes, smokeless tobacco (ST) products still contain nicotine of varying concentrations as well as a number of carcinogens that are just as harmful.

Cigarettes and oral snuff have similar amounts of nicotine (milligrams per gram of tobacco), while chewing tobacco appears to have "somewhat lower" amounts compared with cigarettes, Dr. Piano and her colleagues wrote.

"Even though certain manufacturing techniques are used to reduce the level of these compounds in some products, they remain present in substantial concentrations in ST products, including Swedish snus," they said.

In a comparison of nicotine concentration between three types of smokeless tobacco products (chewing tobacco, dry snuff, and moist snuff) and cigarettes sold in the United States, all of the smokeless tobacco products had nicotine concentrations that were similar to cigarettes with the highest concentrations.

Dr. Piano and her colleagues found that unlike the aforementioned Swedish cohorts, there was no reduction in smoking rates among people in the United States using smokeless tobacco. (The sale of smokeless tobacco products such as moist snuff or snus is banned in most of the European Union with the exception of Sweden and Norway.)

In the United States about 8.1 million people are users of smokeless tobacco and its use is more prevalent in men than women, and people between the ages of 18–25 are the most likely to use smokeless tobacco, the researchers wrote.

It also appears that although U.S. chewing tobacco use has been on the decline since the 1980s, snuff consumption and production are increasing, the researchers said.

| "Smokeless tobacco products are at least
  98 percent safer than smoking."

Smokeless Tobacco Is a Safer, Effective Way to Quit Smoking

Jeff Stier and Brad Rodu

Jeff Stier is associate director of the American Council on Science and Health. Brad Rodu is a professor at the University of Louisville Department of Medicine. In the following viewpoint, the authors claim that the dangers of smokeless tobacco have been exaggerated by politicians and anti-tobacco extremists. Smokeless tobacco is, in fact, a viable form of tobacco harm reduction that has been recognized by prestigious medical organizations, they say. They maintain that studies of Swedish smokers show that smokeless tobacco has been "directly associated with low smoking rates" in Sweden over the last fifty years. Denying smokers safer alternatives, they charge, is immoral.

As you read, consider the following questions:

1. What evidence do the authors provide that abstinence-oriented quitting methods and pharmaceutical nicotine are ineffective at helping smokers?

2. According to the authors, what are the health merits of smokeless tobacco compared to cigarettes?

3. In the authors' view, why are consumers being denied safer alternatives to cigarettes?

"Quit smoking" should be the No. 1 New Year's resolution for 45 million Americans. What a shame if Congress stands in their way. Most smokers know setting tobacco on fire puts their lives in jeopardy, but for them, the risk of dying can't compete with the immediate dread of living without nicotine, a powerfully addictive substance.

Over the last 15 years, 6 million American inveterate smokers—those who couldn't quit—died from lung and other cancers, emphysema, heart disease and stroke. Conventional, abstinence-oriented, quit-smoking tactics don't help inveterate smokers. Pharmaceutical nicotine—in the form of pills, patches and gum—is advertised as a proven and effective cessation aid, but research shows it helps only about 7 percent of smokers. If any other medicine had a success rate that low, it would be labeled a failure. Early this year [2009], if anti-tobacco activists get their way, Congress will pass a tobacco regulation bill that codifies and perpetuates failed tobacco policies. The pending Kennedy/Waxman bill conceals the fact that cigarettes are vastly deadlier than smokeless products and it prohibits manufacturers from truthfully disclosing this marked difference to consumers. The bill ignores science-based tobacco harm reduction involving substituting safer smokeless tobacco products for cigarettes.

Tobacco harm reduction has been enthusiastically endorsed by prestigious medical organizations like the British Royal College of Physicians and the American Association of Public Health Physicians. These societies recognize that smokers who switch to smokeless can achieve almost all the health benefits of tobacco abstinence while obtaining almost all the satisfaction of smoking. Smokeless tobacco products are at least 98 percent safer than smoking. While no tobacco product is completely safe, the majority of cigarette smokers are routinely misinformed—by government agencies and by anti-tobacco extremists—about the relative safety of smokeless products. Unlike cigarettes, smokeless [tobacco] doesn't cause lung cancer, heart disease or emphysema. And what about mouth cancer—a deadly disease commonly linked to smoking? Statistically, users of smokeless tobacco have about the same small risk of dying from mouth cancer as automobile users have of dying in a car wreck.

Tobacco harm reduction has worked in Sweden. For 50 years, smokeless use has been directly associated with low smoking rates there; Swedish men smoke less than those in any other developed country. The result is that Swedish men have the lowest rates of lung cancer and of all smoking-related deaths in the developed world.

And Swedish women are switching too. The reason: Modern smokeless products, available as minipackets or dissolvable pellets of tobacco, can be placed invisibly inside the upper lip, with none of the spit or stigma of old-fashioned chewing tobacco. This month, Congress will have an added incentive to produce legislation to help American smokers: President-elect Barack Obama wants to quit smoking. He is in a position to demand that the bill contain scientifically sound provisions for tobacco harm reduction. As president, he should direct federal agencies to make and keep a New Year's resolution to end the campaign of misinformation that irresponsibly misrepresents scientific information about the use of smokeless products. The Surgeon General, the Centers for Disease Control and Prevention and the National Institutes of Health have been conducting a war against tobacco manufacturers, rather than focusing on proven and practical measures to reduce smokers' risks.

If any other consumer product was as dangerous as cigarettes, society would demand safer alternatives, and it would be scandalous if consumers were denied them. American smokers are literally dying for ways to step away from the fire, and they deserve information about effective, safer smokeless substitutes. Let's give them the facts, and a healthier New Year.

Periodical and Internet Sources Bibliography

The following articles have been selected to supplement the diverse views presented in this chapter.

Thomas Briant	"NATO Opposes Flavored Tobacco and Capsular Ban," *CSP Net,* February 15, 2011.
Steve Chapman	"Tobacco Truth Gets Smoked," *Reason,* January 11, 2010.
Myra Dembrow	"How to Help Patients Stop the Smoking Habit: Chewing Tobacco Should Not Be an Alternative, New Research Confirms," *Clinical Advisor,* January 2008.
Scott Graf	"Electronic Buzz: E-Cigarettes Stir Excitement, Concern," WFAE.org, August 13, 2009.
Nigel Gray and Stephen S. Hecht	"Smokeless Tobacco—Proposals for Regulation," *The Lancet,* vol. 375, no. 9726, May 8, 2010, pp. 1589–1591.
Steve Heilig	"Another Pack of Lies: 'Electronic' Cigarettes, or, a Smoke by Any Other Name," *San Francisco Chronicle,* June 24, 2011.
Patrick McIlheran	"A Smoke Without Exhaust," *Milwaukee-Wisconsin Journal Sentinel,* May 9, 2009.
Reuters	"Snuff Just As Addictive As Cigarettes," MSNBC.com, February 26, 2010.
Jonathan Riskind	"Brown Wants Candy-Like Tobacco Taken off Market," *Columbus Dispatch,* May 2, 2010.
Update	"FDA Takes Action Against Illegal Marketing of Tobacco Products," *PR NewsWire,* May 25, 2011.
David Whelan	"Tobacco Bill Could Snuff out RJR's Smokeless Strategy," *Forbes,* June 1, 2009.

CHAPTER 4

How Do the Media Affect Individuals' Choice to Smoke?

Chapter Preface

In June 2011, the Food and Drug Administration (FDA) unveiled nine new graphic cigarette warning labels as part of the Family Smoking Prevention and Tobacco Control Act signed into law by the President Barack Obama administration two years earlier. Although such warnings have been implemented in a number of countries for decades, they have usually been relegated to fairly simple generalizations ranging from the terse ("Cigarette Smoke Contains Carbon Monoxide") to passive, even innocuous aphorisms such as "The Surgeon General Has Determined That Cigarette Smoking Is Dangerous to Your Health," a label that was discontinued in 1985.

All nine of the new warnings selected by the FDA are the first changes to cigarette packaging to be federally mandated in more than twenty-five years. They are considerably more prominent and deliberately grisly, depicting vivid color graphics of the negative consequences of smoking. The warnings cover fifty percent of the front and rear of each pack, along with supplemental text notable for its equally harsh tautness: "Smoking can kill you;" "Cigarettes are addictive;" "Cigarettes cause fatal lung disease;" and even one urging consumers not to purchase the product at all: "Quitting smoking now greatly reduces serious risks to your health."

Whether illustrations of cancerous lesions, festering lungs, and cratered gums, along with written guarantees of mortality, will be effective at reducing smoking or simply succeed at making smokers feel acute discomfort has yet to be determined. The national smoking cessation hotline 1-800-QUIT-NOW claims that calls more than doubled the day the new packages were revealed to the media, although the actual changes won't appear on retailer shelves until September 2012.

Based on statistics from Canada, which implemented the system a decade ago, the FDA projects that the new labels will reduce the number of smokers by 213,000 in 2013 and lead to subsequent reductions for the next twenty years. However, a study conducted by North Carolina's RTI International (funded by the FDA) casts doubt on the potential impact of the new labels on smokers' decision-making. The authors of the survey found "[t]he graphic cigarette warning labels did not elicit strong responses in terms of intention related to [the] cessation or initiation [of smoking]."

Robert Cunningham, a senior policy analyst at the Canadian Cancer Society, notes that while smoking among Canadian youths indeed showed a sharp drop over the ten-year period cited by the FDA, other factors not easily incorporated, such as increasingly rigid smoking restrictions along with periodic tax hikes, may very well have contributed as much as or more than the graphic warning labels. And while in the FDA study, the labels provoked strong emotional reactions in users, there was little evidence to suggest this led to inspiring them to change their smoking habits or that the imagery would discourage nonsmokers from starting to smoke.

Tobacco manufacturers unsurprisingly oppose the graphic labels, with a spokesman for Reynolds American Inc. noting that the new images "include non-factual cartoon images [and] controversial photographs that appear to have been technologically enhanced to maximize an emotional response."

Just as regulating or compiling data on e-cigarettes has so far proven challenging because of their relative newness and differences from other tobacco products, the jury is simply not yet in on graphic cigarette labels. Even Danny McGoldrick, vice president of research at the Campaign for Tobacco-Free Kids, concedes that the study's accuracy is questionable because it was based entirely on fleeting impressions. "If you see a Nike ad one time," he said, "are you going to go out and buy a pair of shoes?" At the same time, both McGoldrick and Cunningham agree that opposition to the labels by the tobacco companies is proof enough of their efficacy.

Are mandatory labels showing depictions of exaggerated suffering an ingenious way to convey the potential medical consequences of smoking or a misguided effort doomed to backfire with youths savvier and more cynical of marketing gimmickry than previous generations? Or are they simply the inevitable, ironic descendant of the Winston cigarette ads featuring Fred Flintstone that ran free of public or federal outcry on prime time network television in the 1960s?

The viewpoints collected in this chapter will examine how advertisers, manufacturers, legislators, and antismoking activists make selective use of the same data, and explore whether tobacco's role in our culture will endure for years to come or ultimately be snuffed out.

| "*Quantitative studies suggest that youth exposed to on-screen smoking are more likely themselves to initiate smoking.*"

Smoking Should Be Banned from Movies Meant for Youth

Ronald M. Davis, Elizabeth A. Gilpin, Barbara Loken, K. Viswanath, and Melanie A. Wakefield

In the following viewpoint, authors Ronald M. Davis, Elizabeth A. Gilpin, Barbara Loken, K. Viswanath, and Melanie A. Wakefield of the National Cancer Institute argue that tobacco use in movies has led to a long and deliberate spike in youth smoking over the decades, with a long tradition of tobacco companies paying movie studios to feature the use of their products by heroic or sympathetic characters. Consequently, they recommend that any movies showing depictions of smoking be categorically rated R and that such ratings be strictly enforced, including the surveillance of adolescent moviegoers.

As you read, consider the following questions:

1. According to the authors, what is a key concern about depictions of smoking on-screen?

2. What differences did researchers cited in the viewpoint note among college students' reactions to male characters smoking versus female characters smoking?

3. In what way do the authors claim the United States is unique with regard to regulating entertainment content and how do they propose this should affect the handling of scenes involving tobacco consumption?

Examination of the role of entertainment media in tobacco marketing is increasingly becoming an area of active research. Most of this work has focused on portrayal of tobacco in movies. Quantitative studies suggest that youth exposed to on-screen smoking are more likely themselves to initiate smoking. . . .

As [researchers Stanton A.] Glantz and [Jonathan] Polansky argue, there is no evidence that viewers, particularly adolescents, distinguish between portrayals of tobacco in historical, contemporary, and futuristic films or between portrayals of tobacco in American and non-American films to which they are exposed.

The concern about the types of characters who are predominantly depicted as smokers in movies is that smoking is modeled by characters bearing aspirational traits—such as good looks, maturity, affluence, and power—similar to the sorts of images traditionally promoted in tobacco advertisements. Theories of media influence and persuasion predict that role models bearing such traits are the most influential to audiences. . . . Some audience studies suggest that the sheer frequency of exposure (across all movie genres and settings) is important to media impact. Audience studies have not yet examined whether responses vary with the historical setting of smoking. Evidence is emerging, however, that responses vary with character traits of smoking models.

[Researcher A.] McIntosh and colleagues found that in popular films from 1940 to 1989, smokers were depicted as more romantically and sexually active and marginally more intelligent than non-smokers. However, smokers and non-smokers did not differ in terms of their attractiveness, goodness, socioeconomic status, aggressiveness, friendliness, or outcome at film's end. In movies released from 1988 to 1997, smoking often is depicted (1) in association with intimacy and social activity; (2) as motivated by certain mood states (e.g., agitation, sadness, happiness, relaxation, pensiveness); or (3) in conjunction with other risk-taking behaviors (e.g., drug use or violence). Among American movie characters portrayed as contemporary in the 1990s, smoking was more common among antagonists. Two cross-sectional surveys of movie content report that in movies released during the 1990s, smoking was increasingly associated with stress reduction and hostility. It is unclear whether this shift in imagery reflects changes in social norms concerning smoking, cinematic style, or commercial factors.

Health Consequences

A key concern about depictions of smoking on screen is that the health consequences of smoking are rarely shown. Content analyses of children's animated films released between 1937 and 1997 indicated that more than two-thirds of the films included tobacco use without clear verbal messages of any negative long-term health effects of smoking. Similarly, [researcher Anna] Hazan and colleagues found that most tobacco events in movies from 1960 to 1990 did not include health messages. [Researcher Donald] Roberts and others found that, among the 200 most popular movie rentals for 1996 and 1997, negative long-term health effects associated with substance use (smoking, drug use, or alcohol consumption) were rarely depicted (in less than 7% of movies). Similarly, an analysis by [researcher Simon] Everett and colleagues of top box-office U.S. films from 1985 to 1995 indicated that on average only 3.5% of tobacco events were anti-tobacco, compared with 32.3% of tobacco events that were categorized as pro-tobacco. In top-grossing films for 2002, most (92%) incidents involving tobacco were portrayed without consequences.

In another study, youth viewers found that 74% of the top 50 movies between 2000 and 2003 that depicted tobacco contained pro-tobacco messages. [Researcher Matthew] Dalton and colleagues found that negative reactions to tobacco use (e.g., comments about health effects or gestures such as coughing) were depicted in only 6% of tobacco occurrences. [Researcher George] Escamilla and others found that movies rated as PG/PG-13 were less likely than R-rated movies to contain negative messages about smoking. In PG/PG-13 films, only 9 of 22 tobacco messages were anti-tobacco, compared with 21 of 31 messages in R-rated/unrated films. It is especially of concern that health effects may be more frequently omitted from movies targeted toward younger audiences. As demonstrated by social learning theory, showing hazardous behaviors in the absence of negative consequences is likely to make viewers more inclined to mimic them than if the negative consequences were shown.

Brand Appearances

Content analyses suggest that appearances of specific tobacco brands in movies occur frequently, despite a voluntary agreement on the part of the tobacco industry to stop paying for their brands to appear (the Cigarette Advertising and Promotion Code incorporated a voluntary ban on paid product placement circa 1991). In a 10-year sample of top box-office films from 1988 to 1997, the most highly advertised U.S. cigarette brands also accounted for the most brand appearances in the movies, and no decline occurred after 1991. Most (85%) of the films contained some tobacco use, with specific brand appearances in 28% of the total film sample. Brand appearances were as common in films suitable for adolescent audiences as in films for adult audiences. Although 27 tobacco brands were depicted in the movies sampled, 4 cigarette brands accounted for 80% of brand appearances. The brands were Marlboro (40%), Winston (17%), Lucky Strike

(12%), and Camel (11%). Other content analyses of movies sampled from the late 1990s have found that brand appearances for Marlboro occurred five to six times more frequently than those for other tobacco brands. The U.S. film industry's use of the most heavily advertised tobacco brands in internationally distributed films suggests that film serves as a global advertising medium for tobacco, as about one-half of box-office receipts for these films are from overseas.

Often, brand appearances involve only glimpses of cigarette packaging in the ambient scene environment. A subset of brand appearance of particular concern, termed *actor endorsement*, is display of the tobacco brand while an actor handles or uses a product. It is reasonable to single out actor endorsement, because the film industry does so in its negotiations for placements for various products, often asking for a higher payment when an actor uses a particular brand. . . .

Effects of On-Screen Smoking on Viewers' Smoking-Related Beliefs

Theories of media influence predict that role models bearing favored social attributes are likely to be especially persuasive. Several experimental studies have assessed whether stars who smoke on screen promote pro-smoking beliefs among audiences.

Results of experimental studies suggest that viewing movie characters who are smoking enhances viewers' perceptions of how socially acceptable smoking is. [Researchers C.] Pechmann and [C.] Shih found that exposure to movie scenes of popular, young stars smoking (versus non-smoking) prompted adolescent viewers to report that adolescent smokers had higher social stature. This finding was replicated in a second experiment that assessed reactions to a whole movie (*Reality Bites*) depicting smoking compared with an edited version of the movie that excluded smoking depictions. Similarly, [researchers Bryan] Gibson and [John] Maurer found that, among non-smoking college students, viewing a movie clip of a leading male character smoking (versus a comparable clip in which this character does not smoke) resulted in a greater willingness to become friends with a smoker. However, further analyses revealed that this effect was most marked for viewers low on "need for cognition" (a trait predicted to render someone more susceptible to persuasion via the peripheral route). This finding suggests that some people may be more susceptible than others to the persuasive impact of movie depictions of smoking.

[Researcher Harold] Dixon found evidence suggesting that adolescents who watched footage of movie adult characters smoking on screen perceived adult smoking prevalence in the "real world" to be higher than did adolescents who watched footage of non-smoking movie characters. This effect occurred irrespective of the social characteristics of the on-screen smokers that students viewed. Together, these findings suggest that movie depictions of smoking may promote perceptions that smoking is a normative behavior in the real world. These findings are of concern, since social learning variables, "especially peer smoking and approval, prevalence estimates, and offers/availability" have been found to be strongly predictive of smoking onset.

Exposure to on-screen smoking also has been found to influence viewers' beliefs about the social consequences of personal smoking. Pechmann and Shih digitally changed the image frame to edit smoking out of the 1990s film *Reality Bites*. Comparing adolescents' responses to the original versus the non-smoking version of the movie, they found that adolescent never smokers exposed to the original version showed enhanced perceptions of how their social stature would be viewed by others if they were to personally smoke. The video manipulation had no significant effects on participating adolescents' perceptions of how popular, vital, or poised they would look if they were to smoke. Dixon found that beliefs about the social consequences of personal smoking were affected differentially, depending on the social characteristics of the on-screen smoker. Among adolescent viewers, attractive, high-status characters who smoked on screen promoted positive beliefs about the benefits of smoking. However, unattractive, low-status characters who smoked on screen detracted from such beliefs.

Pechmann and Shih also found that exposure to the original version of *Reality Bites* promoted increased personal intentions to smoke among adolescent never smokers. For older viewers, two studies (with sample sizes of 150 or more) found a significant effect of on-screen tobacco depictions on personal intentions to smoke. However, another study (examining a smaller subgroup of 84 non-smokers) did not find such an effect. [Researcher David] Hines and colleagues found that college students who viewed movie scenes in which the main characters smoke were more likely than those who viewed non-smoking scenes to indicate a likelihood to smoke in various situations in which smoking is likely to occur. This effect persisted with controls for the smoking status of the participant. Furthermore, among male viewers who were regular or occasional smokers, the smoking film footage also promoted a higher current desire to smoke. . . .

Effects of Smoking Depictions on General Reactions to Movies

In discussing audience reactions to smoking in movies, it also is relevant to examine responses from the perspective of audiences' entertainment experience. Evidence is mixed as to whether audience perceptions of movie characters are affected by their on-screen smoking. Pechmann and Shih found that, among adolescent never smokers, there were no significant differences in the number of negative, neutral, or positive thoughts about the leading characters in a movie as a function of whether scenes of their smoking were viewed. Similarly, Gibson and Maurer found that, among college students who were non-smokers, viewing movie scenes of a leading male character smoking (versus non-smoking) did not markedly affect their ratings of that character. However, among college students who were smokers, viewing such movie scenes led them to rate the male actor and the character he played as more likeable when he smoked, compared with when he was not depicted as a smoker. Reactions appear to vary, however, depending on the movie character's gender— smoking by females may be associated with negative character traits. Hines and colleagues found that female characters depicted as smokers were rated less favorably on a range of social characteristics (e.g., attractive, sexy, popular), but they found no such effects for male characters. Smoking by female characters also led audience members who were occasional smokers or non-smokers to perceive themselves as less similar to the character. [Researchers Brad] Jones and [Megan] Carroll found that young women who viewed a young female smoking rated her as more outgoing, more sophisticated, not as easy to manipulate, and less emotional about breaking up with her boyfriend than those women who viewed a control video in which the young female did not smoke. In a study examining reactions to different movie character depictions of smokers, Dixon found that adolescents associated smoking by female antagonists with low social status. Ratings of the male characters did not differ in this way. Together, these results suggest that audience members may identify more with movie characters of similar smoking status. Moreover, on-screen smoking by female characters appears to carry some negative social connotations.

Pechmann and Shih found that, in more general reactions to on-screen smoking, viewing movie scenes depicting smoking evoked higher levels of positive arousal than did viewing similar scenes without smoking. Despite the effects of smoking on viewers' emotional arousal, Pechmann and Shih found that adolescents' ratings of a movie's action or storyline or their willingness to recommend the movie to friends was no different for a version of the movie that edited the smoking out of the scene, compared with the original version of the movie. This finding has relevance to filmmakers in suggesting that excluding smoking from films does not detract from their overall appeal. This argument is further corroborated by Dalton and colleagues. They found that the amount of tobacco use depicted in movies is not significantly associated with box-office success. Pechmann and Shih also found that, for adolescent viewers who were shown an anti-smoking advertisement before viewing a movie depicting smoking, the effect of smoking depictions in the movie on arousal, perceptions of a smoker's social stature, and personal intent to smoke were eliminated. This finding and those of [researcher Christine] Edwards and colleagues imply that showing anti-smoking advertisements before movies with smoking could modify the effect of pro-smoking movie depictions on the audience's smoking behavior.

Conclusions Concerning Media Effects Research

The findings from experimental studies contribute to the understanding of how vicarious learning effects may occur in response to smoking behavior symbolically modeled in movies. Along with the results of cross-sectional and longitudinal population-based studies, experimental research indicates that images of smoking in film can influence people's beliefs about social norms for smoking, beliefs about the function and consequences of smoking, and ultimately their personal propensity to smoke. Certain movie depictions may be more likely than others to promote pro-smoking beliefs. Audience members' responsiveness to such imagery may vary as a function of their personal characteristics (especially smoking status and gender). Experimental studies found many statistically significant effects—of a similar magnitude to the effects observed in experimental media research on other health topics—for only brief exposure to movie images of smoking.

Across the different study designs used to assess audience responses to on-screen tobacco use, there is considerable convergence in findings. Pro-tobacco film content has been found to promote pro-smoking beliefs and intentions in both experimental and cross-sectional studies. Exposure to on-screen smoking has been associated with smoking behavior in cross-sectional studies and predictive of smoking behavior in longitudinal studies. A similar convergence of findings across different study types was observed in a meta-analysis examining the effects of media violence on aggression. . . .

Legal/Policy Issues: Artistic or Commercial Speech?

One of the foundations of democratic society involves freedom to express a diversity of views. Expression of diverse viewpoints is valuable for enabling communicators to espouse a cause or position and defend it. The expression of diverse viewpoints provides audiences with material on which to base informed judgments about the world around them. This freedom applies not only to political commentary but also to commentary on behaviors within the culture. Thus, most free societies give artists and other communicators the ability to reflect on, depict, and comment on their perception of the world around them. In the United States, this freedom is incorporated into the constitution as the First Amendment of the Bill of Rights.

Interviews conducted by [researcher David] Shields and colleagues with film industry representatives illustrate the value producers and actors place on freedom of speech and their fears about censorship. The movie industry does not welcome public health strategies that advocate for restricting the freedom to depict tobacco use in its films. However, paid product placement deals between some movie production companies and tobacco companies, and contracts precluding unattractive movie depictions of smoking, reveal that some in the entertainment industry have been compensated by the tobacco industry to add branded smoking and other signage to their artistic output. Given the history of product placement in movies and the similarities between the social imagery of smoking in movies and in tobacco advertising, it is likely that the social iconography of smoking in films derives in large part from images of smoking that the tobacco industry cultivated strategically.

In the past, the American movie industry was not afforded the First Amendment protections it now enjoys in the United States and was subject to censorship at both state and local levels. The movie industry fought censorship, arguing that it interfered with First Amendment speech. But in 1915, in *Mutual Film Corporation v. Industrial Commission of Ohio*, the U.S. Supreme Court determined that motion pictures did not constitute part of the "press" and therefore were not entitled to First Amendment protection from censorship. This case arose in response to the passing of a statute creating a Board of Censors that had to approve all motion pictures prior to their exhibition. Localities continued to censor movies until 1952, when the Supreme Court granted full First Amendment protection to movies in *Joseph Burstyn, Inc. v. Wilson*. At that time, there was little or no product placement in movies, but this is no longer the case. Paid product placement is an integral commercial element in almost every movie. Given the increasing number of product placements in movies, the question is now whether or not depictions of brands in movies should be reclassified as commercial speech, which would be subject to a lower level of First Amendment protection.

Self-regulation by eliminating cigarette brands already is happening in some movie production companies. For example, Robert Reiner requires justification for smoking scenes in movies he produces for Castle Rock Entertainment. As a WHO [World Health Organization] document on this issue states, "The film industry cannot be accused of causing cancer, but they do not have to promote a product that does." In contrast to violence, which may be linked with box-office success, the evidence indicates that the inclusion of smoking is not necessary for the commercial success of movies.

Product placement deals are not the sole reason for on-screen smoking. The decision to portray a character as a smoker may arise from a range of motives, such as a desire to make the character seem realistic, reliance on cigarettes as a prop, and personal smoking behavior of an actor. Nevertheless, movie characters for the most part represent the affluent and most powerful segment of society. When these actors smoke, whether they play the bad or good guy, the risk is that adolescents will emulate the behavior.

Movie Rating Systems

In most countries, movie rating systems exist to protect children from exposure to forms of media society deems harmful or objectionable. The rationale for most rating systems is that society wishes to protect children from seeing media that may have undue influence on their behavior. Most countries have government-sponsored censor boards charged with evaluating the appropriateness of entertainment media for children. The procedures of government-sponsored censor boards are subject to regulation by government and to revision if new data arise regarding a media threat to children. Governments in some countries have attempted to regulate smoking content in entertainment media. In 2001, Russia's lower house of parliament passed a bill to ban images of people smoking in movies and television programs unless smoking is an essential part of the action. The Indian [g]overnment had planned to impose a ban on smoking scenes in new films and television serials in July 2006. Thailand's Film Censorship Board has censored depictions of smoking in movies. For example, the release of the movie *Som and Bank* (*Bangkok for Sale*) was delayed, as the board required that the images of smoking be blurred out. In other countries, efforts are under way to incorporate smoking into government censorship and movie rating systems. For example, the Lung Association in Ontario, Canada, has called upon the government to censor smoking. Some countries also censor aspects of films considered offensive to most adults in their societies. For example, many Arab countries do not allow movies that depict use of tobacco and alcohol to be shown in public places, because doing so violates mainstream religious beliefs.

Because of unique protections on First Amendment speech in the United States, this country does not have censor boards. Instead, the United States is the only country that allows its film industry to rate its own motion pictures. Rating is done through the MPAA. This rating system, established in November 1968, has undergone only minor changes. In the voluntary MPAA rating system, most producers allow their films to be subjected to review by a rating board. Movies are rated primarily according to what the board determines parents would find objectionable (or what Congress might regulate). In its explanation of the ratings system, the MPAA lists violence, nudity, sensuality, language, and drug use as factors the board considers when rating movies. Board members must have parental experience, and the board president is chosen by the MPAA's president. The MPAA and the National Association of Theater Owners [NATO] presidents jointly set decisions regarding rating criteria.

The MPAA promotes the ratings system as a guide to parents. Some might argue that the real purpose of the voluntary movie ratings system is to protect the studios from more intrusive government regulation. In that regard, the film industry has operated in much the same way as the tobacco and alcoholic beverage industries, with the former changing its voluntary rating standard, the Cigarette Advertising and Promotion Code, only when Congress was considering stricter regulations. . . .

Before describing efforts by some in the movie industry to limit the depiction of smoking, it is necessary to describe the industry. Although the industry changes from year to year with buyouts and mergers, the U.S. film industry in 2004 was organized around seven major production companies that finance and distribute motion pictures: Buena Vista Pictures (Disney), Sony Pictures, Metro-Goldwyn-Mayer, Paramount Pictures, Twentieth Century Fox, Universal City Studios, and Warner Brothers Entertainment. Many of the names seen in movies are subsidiaries of these companies. For example, Miramax is a subsidiary of Buena Vista Pictures. These large studios hire production executives responsible for financing their major in-house movie efforts. Many independent film producers also make movies. For independent movies to be successful, the producer must partner with one of the major studios for the widespread distribution of the film. Other players in the industry (the artists) are organized through guilds, bodies that serve as financial advocates for their constituents (directors, actors, screenwriters, etc.) in much the same way that labor unions act on behalf of their members.

The MPAA represents the domestic interests of the major studios, and the Motion Picture Association represents the international interests. The president of the MPAA is also the chief lobbyist for the industry in Washington, D.C. When approached by the state attorneys general in August 2003, Jack Valenti, the MPAA president at the time, sponsored a series of meetings that included himself, the NATO president, and various guilds. However, Valenti declined to incorporate smoking into the MPAA rating system. Four years later, in February 2007, the Harvard School of Public Health recommended that the MPAA take action to "eliminate the depiction of tobacco smoking from films accessible to children and youth." In May 2007, 31 attorneys general wrote a letter to major movie studio heads supporting this recommendation and stating the dangers of exposing children to smoking depictions in movies. In a response released that same month, former congressman Dan Glickman, Valenti's successor as president of MPAA, stated that the MPAA would begin to consider smoking depictions when rating movies. However, a letter to the MPAA in June of 2007 from U.S. senators [Dick] Durbin, [Ted] Kennedy, and [Frank] Lautenberg described MPAA's new policy as "not enough to curb the influence of smoking in the movies on the health of children." Six months after the new policy began, Polansky, Glantz, and Titus reported that there was no substantial change in the percentage of G, PG, or R-rated movies that included smoking depictions compared with the same time period in each of the four previous years. . . .

Smoke Free Movies and the Rate Smoking "R" Public Health Campaign

Smoke Free Movies is a public health campaign started by Stanton A. Glantz in 2001. The campaign aims to reduce the impact of smoking in movies on adolescents through four specific, voluntary changes in movie industry policy:

Rate new smoking movies R. Any film that shows or implies tobacco use should be rated R. The only exceptions should be when the presentation of tobacco clearly and unambiguously reflects the dangers and consequences of tobacco use or is necessary to represent smoking by a real historical figure.

Certify no payoffs. The producers should post a certificate in the credits at the end of the movie declaring that nobody on the production received anything of value (cash money, free cigarettes or other gifts, free publicity, interest-free loans, or anything else) from anyone in exchange for using or displaying tobacco or its use.

Require strong anti-smoking advertisements. Studios and theaters should require a genuinely strong anti-smoking advertisement (not one produced by a tobacco company) to run before any film with any tobacco presence, regardless of its MPAA rating.

Stop identifying tobacco brands. There should be no tobacco brand identification and no presence of tobacco brand imagery (such as billboards) in the background of any movie scene.

The aim of the Smoke Free Movies campaign is to create a groundswell of support for these policy aims within the public health community and, eventually, among public policymakers to bring pressure to bear on the industry. By 2004, the campaign gained the endorsement of many mainstream health organizations, including WHO, the American Medical Association, the American Academy of Pediatrics, and the American Heart

Association. The Smoke Free Movies media campaign began by rolling out a controversial print advertising campaign in March 2001 that was aimed at members of the movie industry. The campaign was designed to raise awareness about the effect of smoking in movies on adolescent smoking; to place responsibility for change on studio executives, theater owners, and actors; and to suggest government oversight. Along with the advertising campaign, Smoke Free Movies has organized and maintains a network of public health activists at state and local levels. These groups have developed awareness campaigns aimed at youth (in New York, Texas, and Vermont, among others), have engaged in a national letter-writing campaign to movie stars, and have encouraged other forms of activism, such as e-mail messages to movie executives.

The most controversial policy aim of Smoke Free Movies is the R rating for smoking. This policy aim has been under the control of the movie studios and theater owners, the two entities that run the MPAA rating system. From the original perspective of the movie industry, the movie rating system was designed for concerned parents and was not designed in relation to public health considerations. However, the ratings do include violence. After the Columbine High School shootings in 1999, public health considerations were added when efforts by President [Bill] Clinton, the Senate, and public health experts led to changes in the movie industry's depiction of violence in R-rated films. The movie industry deleted the most violent scenes from soon-to-be released films and increased restrictions on how R-rated movies are marketed. From a public health perspective, limiting the portrayal of tobacco in movies is important because of its link to adolescent smoking (see earlier discussion) and the severity of the health consequences of smoking compared with some other depictions of behavior (e.g., using foul language).

Another issue that has been raised is whether the balance between adolescents' desire to see R-rated movies and parental attempts to limit viewing of these movies weighs in favor of higher or lower exposure rates for R-rated movies among young adolescents. If adolescents successfully circumvent attempts by parents and theaters to restrict their exposure to these movies, their viewing rates would be expected to be similar to other rating categories. The R rating for the smoking campaign, in this case, would be futile and possibly even counterproductive. If view rates for R-rated movies are in fact lower among young adolescents, then the argument could be made that rating movies with smoking R could limit adolescent exposure despite making them "forbidden fruit." . . .

Would the R rating for smoking have a substantial immediate impact on adolescents' exposure to smoking in movies? Smoke Free Movies is calling for the R rating to be applied only to new movies. Most adolescents' exposure to R movies is through seeing older movies on video and DVD. The prospective R rating for smoking would therefore substantially cut exposure to depictions of smoking at theaters that air new releases and would have a more pronounced impact over time because of the cumulative effects of the rating change. On the other hand, if the R rating for smoking caused parents to pay less attention to the ratings system, it could result in the reach of R-rated movies increasing among younger adolescents. Because of these concerns, it may be wise to also consider, along with implementation of this policy change, surveillance of R-rated movie viewership among adolescents and inclusion of a motivational effort to convince parents to take the ratings system literally and seriously.

| *"Smoking in movies is a problem. So what might be done about it?"*

Regulations to Address Smoking in Films Are Largely Misguided

Simon Chapman

Simon Chapman is a professor at the School of Public Health in Sydney, Australia. In the following viewpoint, Chapman considers the presence of smoking in movies an issue worthy of discussion, but one too complex to be remedied simply by banning smoking from movies altogether. Chapman argues that such "throwing out the baby with the bathwater" strategies would tar otherwise exemplary films with the same brush, and that portraying life so unrealistically would hamper the art form as well as the message. Chapman also suggests that automatically giving any movie with smoking in it regardless of context an R rating or pixilating the cigarettes would also serve no useful purpose. In his view, smoking should be handled carefully and with realism, and ratings for movies should be judged, as they already are in other areas, on a case-by-case basis.

As you read, consider the following questions:

1. In the author's view, what is the discrepancy observed in

the organization Smoke Free Movies' concession to allow exceptions for "real historical figures" who smoked?

2. Why does the author consider R-rating all movies with smoking in them untenable?

3. How does the author justify his assertion that tobacco control has long had a "slippery slope" problem?

In 1997 Ron Davis, *Tobacco Control*'s inaugural editor, and I wrote an editorial titled "Smoking in movies: is it a problem?" Since then, a growing body of research has examined the relation between viewing of movies containing depictions of smoking and subsequent smoking among youth. Reviewing this evidence, a 2008 National Cancer Institute monograph concluded "The depiction of cigarette smoking is pervasive in movies, occurring in three-quarters or more of contemporary box-office hits. Identifiable cigarette brands appear in about one-third of movies. The total weight of evidence from cross-sectional, longitudinal and experimental studies indicates a causal relationship between exposure to depictions of smoking in movies and youth smoking initiation." The report's conclusion is consistent with common sense and should give major impetus to what is a growing debate. If the highly choreographed imagery of tobacco advertising influences the uptake of smoking, then so will widespread positive depictions of smoking in movies, now arguably rivalling direct tobacco advertising as the world's largest vector for sustaining the appeal of smoking. Smoking in movies *is* a problem.

So what might be done about it? Many nations ban all tobacco advertising because of its influence on smoking. The idea that movies with smoking scenes should similarly be either banned or at least regulated through adult-only classification has gained traction in a small number of nations, particularly India, Thailand and the United States. The debate remains nascent elsewhere, with few signs of government interest.

In this commentary, I critically review three of the most prominent strategies proposed as ways of controlling smoking in movies. I caution that banning smoking from movies constitutes a fundamental threat to freedom of expression, inviting unavoidable ridicule for the inconsistencies and "airbrushing of reality" that its adoption would unleash. This is likely to alienate many ordinary and influential people who would otherwise be strongly supportive of comprehensive and tough tobacco control. I conclude that nations should pass or amend laws to require "no product placement" disclosures; global efforts should be increased to expose the extent and consequences of smoking in movies; and whistleblowers should be encouraged to expose instances of tobacco industry inducements to the movie industry so that prosecutions can arise where possible. Efforts should continue to persuade directors to be more judicious in their use of gratuitous smoking where this is unnecessary to the verisimilitude of their productions. And finally, smoking should become *one* element taken into account in film classification, but as occurs now with film rating classification in relation to other adult elements, it should be considered in overall context on a case-by-case basis rather than triggering automatic upward classification.

Is Tobacco Product Placement Still Occurring?

Movies have long been prized vehicles for manufacturers to promote their products. When prominent actors smoke in box office hits, powerful and indelible associations are added to smoking. Globally, hundreds of millions of young people view these movies every year, often regardless of their rating status. No one should therefore be surprised that the tobacco industry has a long history of promoting both smoking and particular brands by inducing producers to show products in the hands and between the lips of leading actors. While the US-based tobacco industry has denied since 1990 that it continues product placement in movies, and the 1998 Master Settlement Agreement, which the major companies have signed, expressly outlaws the practice, few experienced with the tobacco industry's track record trust these assurances. Orthodox tobacco promotional avenues are being closed through spreading national advertising bans and the tobacco industry actively exploits legislative loopholes in new media. It would therefore be astonishing if tobacco interests were not still surreptitiously funding movie producers via third parties to have actors smoke in movies with major appeal to the industry's most important market segments, especially youth.

If this could be shown to be occurring in the United States, it would be simply another form of tobacco advertising, breaching undertakings in the Master Settlement Agreement. If occurring in movie production in the increasing number of nations with laws incorporating comprehensive definitions of what constitutes tobacco advertising, it would be prosecutable. Yet no such prosecutions have occurred. If paid product placement is indeed ongoing and as widespread as some tobacco control advocates imply, with myriads of directors insisting that actors smoke, it is also significant that no whistleblowers have emerged with examples of recent movies in which such inducements occurred. The movie industry contains many powerful individuals who would be appalled by such activity and who doubtless would like to expose such conduct if indeed it were happening.

Some tobacco control advocates see a movie cigarette and conclude "tobacco industry!" Sometimes it may well be, but often it is not, anymore than every time we see a car in a movie we should feel obliged to conclude "automobile industry!" People smoke, just as people drive, drink and eat. Filmmakers reflect this.

An equally plausible explanation for smoking in movies, therefore, is that many movie directors are attuned to the richly signifying semiotics of smoking and often judge that characters should smoke to convey particular associations. Here the options for control are far more complex. Three broad approaches have been proposed to reduce minors' exposure to smoking scenes in movies: banning all scenes of smoking (proposed, but now dormant after widespread opposition in India); de facto banning through pixilating the act of smoking and packs of cigarettes (Thailand); and one which appears to have the widest support—introducing an "R" classificatory rating either via movie industry voluntary codes or by law, preventing children under 17 years from admission to movies depicting smoking unless accompanied by an adult (this is the US guideline). Stan Glantz's Smoke Free Movies website proposes an R rating thus: "Any film that shows or implies tobacco should be rated 'R.' The only exceptions should be when the presentation of tobacco clearly and unambiguously reflects the dangers and consequences of tobacco use or is necessary to represent the smoking of a real historical figure."

Banning All Smoking in Movies?

Film, the internet, magazines, literature and newspapers have a long history of being seen by various interest groups—political, moral/religious and health—as vehicles that carry a diverse range of pernicious content said to be harmful to those exposed to it. Nations adopt a range of policies toward such content ranging from massive state control of all content (for example, North Korea and Myanmar (Burma) through to large-scale active and passive censorship of material that offends political or religious sensibilities, as occurs routinely in many despotic, authoritarian and religiously fundamentalist nations.

At the opposite end of such policy are nations where freedom of speech and expression are enshrined as being of fundamental importance to the social and political fabric. In such nations, censorship—for whatever noble purpose—is met with principled resistance with the onus being on those demanding censorship to demonstrate that the case for intervention is strong, and that the consequences of exposure are very serious. The few examples here are absolute prohibitions on promoting terrorism and producing or displaying child pornography, and on the overt incitement of violence and racial vilification.

Those who see movies as essentially vehicles for the transmission of health authority-sanctioned content meet opposition from those who argue that the role of film in open societies is far wider than being simply a means of mass communication of desirable or healthy role models to young people. Many movies depict social problems, people behaving badly and the seamy side of life.

The role of cinema and literature is not simply to promote overtly pro-social or health "oughts" but to have people also reflect on what "is" in society or in screenwriters' imaginations. This includes a long list of disturbing, anti-social, dangerous and unhealthy realities. Numbered among these are domestic violence, animal cruelty, the exploitation of minorities, injustice, and neglect. Whether for educational purpose, entertainment or the broader purpose of artistic expression, filmmakers have often depicted highly socially undesirable activities such as racial hatred and vilification (for example, *Schindler's List*, *Mississippi Burning*), genocide (*Hotel Rwanda*), gang violence (*Romper Stomper*, *Clockwork Orange*) and crime (choose from literally thousands). It would be ridiculously simplistic to assume that by showing something most would regard as undesirable, a filmmaker's purpose was always to endorse such activity. People learn in ways far more complex than being fed a continuous diet of wholesome role models. Many would deeply resent a view of movies that saw them as the equivalent of religious or moral instruction, to be controlled by those inhabiting the same values.

Moreover, hundreds of millions of people around the world smoke. It would be unprecedented for cinema to have to "pretend" that this reality was not the case by never showing smoking in any movie, thereby implying that it was as heinous as (for example) child pornography, but less of a problem than the commonplace murder, mayhem and violence seen in countless films. It would invite ridicule from many people within and beyond the health sector, who would see such a proscription on showing or mentioning smoking as an affront to freedom of speech. It is undoubtedly for this reason that the only nation that has sought to actually ban all smoking from movies (India) met with principled and successful resistance, including from many within the Indian civil society and arts communities.

Smoke Free Movies' concession that exceptions should be allowed for "real historical figures" who smoked (such as [British prime minister Winston] Churchill or [Chinese Communist leader] Mao Tse-Tung) in R-rating is notable here. It acknowledges that cinema should not "airbrush" historical reality. What is left unexplained here, though, is why it is permissible for children to see known historical smokers smoking, but not smokers set in a period such as the 1950s when the reality of social life was that smoking was widespread and unrestricted. Or indeed, why it would not equally be airbrushing of reality to show smoking in a movie set today depicting a group of people from a social or cultural group where smoking was the norm and therefore an accurate aspect of their lives?

Pixilating Smoking in Movies?

Thai law requires that any movie or programme broadcast on television showing cigarettes or smoking must pixilate the cigarettes. The reasoning here would appear to be that as long as people do not actually see a cigarette, somehow the normative message will not get through to audiences. Bungon Ritthiphakdee, a Thai tobacco control expert, says that local television, movie and drama producers today seldom script scenes of people smoking since the law was introduced, because the required pixilation adds an extra production cost and, more importantly, annoys viewers. Pixilation is therefore today largely confined to foreign produced, imported films.

Pixilation is common practice on television news crime reports: innocent until found guilty felons' faces are pixilated as they enter court before a trial. But is there anyone who doesn't think "there's the felon!" just as a pixilated cigarette would not immediately tell viewers that here was someone smoking? It is difficult to imagine what Thai health authorities think that not actually *seeing* the cigarette will achieve.

R-Rate All Smoking Scenes?

In many liberal societies, sexual, violent and illicit drug scenes in movies invoke classification as unsuitable for very young children, although there is considerable variation between nations about what is permissible to screen to children. Parents do not have time to research the content of all movies and value movie classifications as a way of helping them avoid inappropriate, possibly disturbing, content. This brings us to the widely supported proposal that smoking should not be banned in movies, but that all but manifestly anti-smoking scenes—even those where smoking is only "implied"—should cause a movie to be classified as "R." Under the Smoke Free Movies policy, this would mean that even *one* instance of smoking would see a movie classified as being equivalent to the Motion Picture Association of America's standard for those depicting "adult themes, adult activity, hard language, intense or persistent violence, sexually-oriented nudity, drug abuse or other elements," where such scenes are often sustained. Is this an equivalence that many in the community would find reasonable?

For example, the US-based Smoke Free Movies site currently rates the new Batman movie *The Dark Knight* as "promoting smoking" because, amid a cast of thousands, one minor character smokes a cigar. While activists dedicated to eradicating smoking in children's movies engage in organised complaining about such closely monitored incidents, it seems improbable that many ordinary citizens would spontaneously rise up in community protest about such minor usage in the way they would about the sort of sustained adult content that currently sees movies classified as unsuitable for children, should those movies be not so classified. In this respect, arguments based on the unacceptability to the community of *any* smoking scenes are highly unlikely to find widespread support and be seen as overly extreme solutions proposed by single-minded interest groups.

Slippery Slope Problems?

In tobacco control, "slippery slope" or "thin end of the wedge" arguments have a long and disreputable history. For many years the tobacco industry used such arguments to trivialise the health risks of smoking, arguing (for example) that if health warnings were to go on cigarette packs, then they should also go on a large range of other ordinary products that might be harmful too, despite these often being of incomparably lower risk. Such sophistry, however, does not mean that problems of inconsistency are not problematic to the determination of reasonable social policy. If even a single instance of smoking were to consign a movie to R status because of its potential to influence children to smoke, immediate parallel questions arise about a wide range of other potentially adverse role modelling cues in films.

Smoking causes massive health problems, but in that it is not unique. Globally, large-scale health and social problems flow from many activities that also often appear in movies. These include crime, physical inactivity, over-eating, excessive use of alcohol, unsafe sex, speeding and dangerous driving, gambling, risk taking such as extreme sport and adventure, motor cycle use and helmet-less cycling. For example, by the same reasoning that movies showing smoking might normalise or glamorise tobacco use, it could be argued that film should never show positive scenes of gluttony or actors enthusiastically eating fast food because of the obesity epidemic and millions of overweight and obese children struggling to control their weight. Countless comedy scripts would need to go back to the drawing board. Scenes of people drinking alcohol might be excised from children's movies—particularly if those drinking seemed to be enjoying it—because this might seed inappropriate ideas about alcohol in tender minds. All car chases and speeding scenes of course would be restricted to adult movies.

Smoking cartoon characters have been fingered as unacceptable and a smoking Babar the elephant and a pipe smoking Santa Claus have been condemned. So by the same concerns, why not also R-rate the maniacal *Road Runner*, whose disrespect for the highway code might be taken literally by the same innocent children?

These examples are not either facetious or hypothetical, but invite an "alphabet soup" of classificatory ratings, all respectful of the cases that could be mounted by other single issue health and social problem interest groups. For example, in August 2008, Dr. Martin Schiff, a US weight-loss expert called for movies promoting obesity to be classified "O" (for obesity): "Every day we see examples of overeating, gorging, food play and general disregard for health in movies and TV shows. No wonder millions of people are overweight." He nominated the family-oriented Abba musical *Mamma Mia!* for an "O" rating because it contained scenes of a lavish party and feast "where the participants seem to be eating anything and everything."

Most will dismiss such calls as entirely unreasonable. But an illustration of how such inconsistency plays out in practice comes from scenesmoking.org, which rates the 2008 *What Happens in Vegas*, starring Cameron Diaz, as a "thumbs up/pink lung" because it contains no smoking. However, it does contain binge drinking, failure to wear seat belts, intoxication leading to possibly unprotected sex, gambling and a parody of spousal abuse. With such a film receiving a ringing endorsement from this youth-friendly organisation, ordinary people might be entitled to ask about consistency.

If R-rating proponents succeeded in having all smoking scenes restricted to R-rated movies, would this keep most children from seeing them? Hardly, as children's access to R-rated and even X-rated movies is widespread. A recent study showed that all 40 extremely violent movies were seen by a median of

12.5% of US adolescents aged 10–14 years. *Blade, Training Day*, and *Scary Movie* were seen, respectively, by 37.4%, 27.3% and 48.1% of the overall sample and 82.0%, 81.0% and 80.8% of black male adolescents. R-rating[s] may deplete box office takings, as R-rated movies are known to attract smaller audiences, but with rentals and downloaded movies easily accessible to children, it is doubtful whether fewer children in total would see them.

Do All Scenes Promote Smoking?

Another problem with R-rating movies with any smoking scenes other than those that openly proselytise against smoking in Surgeon General warning style, lies with R-classification proponents' beliefs that all depictions of smoking are self-evidently alluring, which is why they need classifying for adults only. This is a simplistic notion that could result in some powerful anti-smoking messages being kept away from children.

Consider two examples. An ongoing story line from the immensely popular American TV series *Friends* (51 million watched the final episode in the US alone) featured the character Chandler's attempts to quit smoking. Scenes included showing him smoking but the overall narrative was anti-smoking, despite scenes and lines often talking about the attractions of smoking. Any rule relegating any smoking to R would see children deprived of the benefit of seeing such memorable indictments of smoking. Those who want to banish such scenes from young eyes can thereby score some own-goals.

In *In Her Shoes*, starring Cameron Diaz, Toni Collette and Shirley MacLaine, Diaz plays the insect thin, dyslexic, rudderless younger sister of Collette's character. They have had an emotional roller-coaster of a childhood, and the film takes us through an emotional resolution as they become re-acquainted with their estranged grandmother (MacLaine). At one stage, Diaz reaches for a cigarette. The sagacious MacLaine says "you shouldn't smoke. You have a history of lung cancer in your family." MacLaine takes the cigarette away, as a grandmother can.

If the movement to get all non-historical depictions of smoking R-certificated succeeds, then this powerful moment would relegate the film to R-rating (supposing that its other content had not already caused this). If that happened, then perhaps many thousands of young people around the world, lured by Diaz's box office appeal, would be denied the richly contextualised and powerful message that the movie delivers: people who smoke are often very glamorous and cool, and drip with "attitude" but, like Diaz, they are often drifting, confused, and in the end, not particularly attractive characters. Why try to keep all this away from adolescents?

Such films present richly textured moral tales for young people to absorb and reflect on as they form their values and make decisions about matters like smoking. Only the crudest of early "hypodermic" media effects models could posit that a single glimpse of smoking will, Pied Piper fashion, lure children ineluctably into a life of smoking. Film classification panels understand the importance of context in assigning their classifications, and are unlikely to be convinced that even one glimpse of smoking in any film is so self-evidently unacceptable that such an inflexible formulaic approach is justified.

The Smoke Free Movies project specifies an exemption for smoking scenes "when the presentation of tobacco clearly and unambiguously reflects the dangers and consequences of tobacco use." This also seems an overly narrow guideline. For example, a family movie which featured an ongoing narrative about a mother struggling to quit, whose smoking upset her family, which saw the character exiled from friends by having to smoke in alleyways outside restaurants, and who expressed regret about having commenced could send a powerful anti-smoking message which would fall well short of the prescribed "health consequences" message.

For many years, tobacco control laboured to free itself from its early moralistic associations with dour temperance-based movements, close brethren of movements which routinely protested at licentious literature and film, modern dancing and other devil's work. In the United States, there is some evidence that R-ratings for smoking in the manner described have substantial community support. But the United States is a nation with a broad rump of historical puritanism that is less evident in many nations. The mere popularity of a proposal should also not blind us to its shortcomings. Overly prescriptive, absolutist hostility to any sight of smoking in movies risks rekindling these historical associations, which may alienate many otherwise strong supporters of tobacco control and stimulate bitingly sarcastic diversions that could be avoided by more reasonable case-by-case policy.

What Should Be Done?

There are legally important differences between commercial speech (such as advertising) and free speech of the sort contained in cultural expression like movies and literature, and any attempt to equate them as a basis for regulation, particularly on the basis of mere suspicion that the tobacco industry must be directing smoking scene traffic, will fail in most nations. But where product placement can be shown to be a direct result of tobacco industry promotional efforts, the matter crosses the line.

Whistleblowers have made invaluable contributions to tobacco control. Potential informants should be actively fostered to speak out about product placement and legal action taken against any companies found to be engaging in it for having broken the Master Settlement Agreement ("No Participating Manufacturer may, beginning 30 days after the MSA Execution Date, make, or cause to be made, any payment or other consideration to any other person or entity to use, display, make reference to or use as a prop any Tobacco Product, Tobacco Product package, advertisement for a Tobacco Product, or any other item bearing a Brand Name in any motion picture, television show, theatrical production or other live performance, live or recorded performance of music, commercial film or video, or video game."). Governments around the world should explicitly incorporate similar clauses in their tobacco advertising legislation.

The growing momentum of evidence so thoroughly summarised in the National Cancer Institute report should be publicised widely, with particular efforts to do this within the movie industry. This will accelerate critical discourse within the industry, which can only heighten awareness about its role in promoting smoking. Smoke Free Movies' efforts in this regard are exemplary although, as I have argued, likely to be generating unnecessary resistance from many because of their overly absolutist guidelines that all smoking, no matter how fleeting, should trigger an R-rating.

Concerns that outright bans on smoking in movies "airbrush reality" raise the serious concerns I have outlined. But equally serious is the paucity of movies where the health consequences of smoking are even mentioned, let alone dramatised. This is airbrushing in the opposite direction. Here, tobacco control advocates should not insist that all movies with smokers be obliged to show its consequences, because such insistence erroneously assumes that movies are essentially health promotion vehicles requiring sign-off from health panels. Adolescents who smoke very rarely get sick and die in adolescence, so such an insistence would throw up the ridiculous spectre of all such films having to add an epilogue showing what happened to the smokers in later life. But the public health community could encourage writers and directors to engage with health consequence subplots more often than they do now. Many social movements have successfully partnered with the movie industry to increase exposure to their issues.

The discourse about the responsibility of directors has already had an impact within the industry. The Walt Disney company's decision to no longer include any smoking in its family viewing fare will see the demise of the odd cigar-chomping pirate in such movies. Few could object to such gestures. But few sensible people see the problem as being much to do with the occasional sight of a cigarette or pipe in overtly "family entertainment." The major challenge comes with adolescent-targeted movies where smoking can have a major presence. As I have argued, it is difficult to be categorical that *any* smoking in a movie must mean that *all* such movies "promote" smoking.

But it is undeniable that many such movies do, with the exact same consequences for the health of millions that were invoked as justification for controlling tobacco advertising. If the more reasonable proposition were promoted that smoking ought to be considered as *one* element within movie rating panels' assessments of how a movie should be rated, I would predict that many within government and the movie industry would be more receptive and more progress would be made.

> "Health warning labels on tobacco products constitute the most cost-effective tool for educating smokers and non-smokers alike about the health risks of tobacco use."

Adding More Graphic Warnings to Cigarette Packs Is an Effective Antismoking Deterrent

Geoffrey T. Fong, David Hammond, and Sara C. Hitchman

Geoffrey T. Fong, David Hammond, and Sara C. Hitchman are professors of psychology at the University of Waterloo. The authors of the following viewpoint argue that adding more graphic warnings to cigarette packs should be encouraged. They maintain that such warnings have already been proven to be a successful antismoking deterrent in the past, especially in countries where the literacy rate is exceptionally low and where the populace has little access to medical information. The authors claim that smokers themselves statistically favor more health information on cigarette packaging in general.

As you read, consider the following questions:

1. What three benefits of pictorial warnings on cigarettes packs do the authors claim have been demonstrated in research studies conducted in the European Union?

2. Why do the authors contend that pictorial warnings are particularly important when communicated to populations with lower literacy rates and what caveat to such methods do they maintain is "critical" to bear in mind?

3. What are two methods cited by the authors that several countries are exploring to enhance the effectiveness of pictorial warnings?

Health warning labels on tobacco products constitute the most cost-effective tool for educating smokers and non-smokers alike about the health risks of tobacco use. In many countries, more smokers report getting information about the health risks of smoking from warning labels than any other source except television. Additionally, non-smokers, including children, report high awareness of warning labels.

Theories in social and health psychology, supported by empirical studies, have demonstrated the superiority of using pictures and imagery over text-only messages in health communication. Since the 1950s, many research studies have demonstrated that "fear appeals" are effective in motivating health behaviour change (e.g., quitting), especially if paired with information about how to avoid the fearful consequences (e.g., where to find help about quitting).

Effectiveness of Warnings

Evidence for the greater potential impact of pictorial warnings have come from focus groups and interview studies, experimental exposure studies and population-based surveys among Canadian smokers, Australian youth, Dutch smokers and from several countries of the 20-country ITC Project: prospective cohort surveys of adult smokers in Australia, Canada and the United States of America (USA), smokers in New Zealand, smokers in Canada and Mexico, smokers and youth in Malaysia and Thailand. In addition to the ITC surveys, there are other research studies that support the use of pictorial warnings, notably in the European Union. Taken as a whole, the research on pictorial warnings show that they are: (i) more likely to be noticed than text-only warning labels; (ii) more effective for educating smokers about the health risks of smoking and for increasing smokers' thoughts about the health risks; and (iii) associated with increased motivation to quit smoking.

A recent analysis of data from the ITC Four Country Survey compared the impact of the introduction of pictorial warnings in Australia in 2005 to that of the introduction of larger text-only warnings in the United Kingdom in 2003. Cognitive and behavioral indicators of label impact that are predictive of quit intentions and quit attempts (e.g., forgoing cigarettes because of the labels; thinking about the health risks of smoking) increased to a greater extent among smokers after the Australian pictorial warnings were introduced than they did in the United Kingdom after enhanced text-only warnings were introduced. Pictorial warnings are also cited by former smokers as an important factor in their attempt to quit and have been associated with increases in the use of effective cessation services, such as toll-free telephone "helplines." Although all warnings are subject to wear-out over time, pictorial warnings have also been shown to sustain their effects longer than text-only warning labels.

Pictorial warnings may be particularly important in communicating health information to populations with lower literacy rates. This is particularly important considering that, in most countries, smokers report lower levels of education than the rest of the population. Preliminary evidence also suggests that countries with pictorial warnings demonstrate fewer disparities in health knowledge across educational levels. It should be noted that particular care should be taken in the selection of

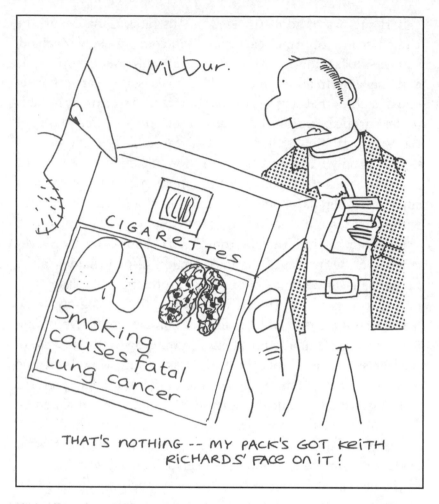

That's nothing... my pack's got Keith Richard's face on it," cartoon by Dawbarn Wilbur. www
.CartoonStock.com. Copyright © Dawburn Wilbur. Reproduction rights obtainable from
www.CartoonStock.com.

pictures for use in low literacy populations: without supporting
text, pictures of smoking could inadvertently suggest approval
rather than warning of its harms. Although pictures may say a
thousand words, it is critical to select those that say the correct
thousand words.

Evidence from low- and middle-income countries also supports the effectiveness of large pictorial warnings over text-only

warnings, and even suggests that pictorial warnings may be even more effective in these countries because warning labels represent one of the few sources of information about the health risks of smoking (in some countries, warnings are the only systematic source of such information). In 2006, Thailand implemented new warning labels that included graphic pictures at the top 50% of the package. After implementation of these new warnings, the percentage of Thai smokers stating that the labels made them think about the health risks increased and as did the percentage of those saying the labels made them more likely to quit. A survey that was conducted in Malaysia—where the text-only warning labels did not change—showed no such increases. These findings have also been replicated among nationally representative samples of youth in Malaysia and Thailand. An ITC experimental study among Chinese smokers, non-smokers and youth in four cities provides strong support for the use of pictorial warnings. Pictorial warnings were rated by all groups as being more effective than text-only warning labels for motivating smokers to quit, convincing youth not to start and informing the public of the dangers of smoking.

No Adverse Consequences

The tobacco industry has suggested that the use of large pictures may reduce the effectiveness of health warnings and could actually lead to increases in smoking behaviour. This is captured in a quotation from the former chief executive officer of British American Tobacco: "The growing use of graphic image health warnings . . . can offend and harass consumers—yet in fact give them no more information than print warnings." However, there is no evidence that pictorial warnings lead to boomerang effects. An analysis of data from the ITC Four Country Survey found that the Australian pictorial warnings, introduced in 2005, led to greater avoidant behaviours (e.g., covering up the pack, keeping it out of sight, or avoiding particular labels), compared to Canada, the United Kingdom, and the

USA. Importantly, those smokers who engaged in avoidant behaviours were no less likely to intend to quit or to attempt to
quit, replicating the findings of a study of the Canadian warnings. Thus, although pictorial warnings can lead to avoidance
and defensive reactions, such reactions are actually indicators
of positive impact.

Research shows that smokers want to see more health information on cigarette packages. Data from ITC surveys of smokers
from 10 countries in 2006 shows that the percentage of smokers who want to see more information on cigarette packages is
greater than the percentage of smokers who want to see less information—even in countries where pictorial warning labels had
already been introduced.

Several countries are exploring methods to enhance the effectiveness of pictorial warnings, including warnings that are
directly informed by research on the neuropsychology of emo-
tion to maximize negative emotional arousal (Brazil), testimo-
nial warnings that depict real people (Chile), strategies to make
cessation and supportive information more engaging (e.g.,
through the inclusion of a "quitline" telephone number, as in
New Zealand) and the addition of a mass media campaign that
synergistically uses themes and images from the set of pictorial
warnings to build strength across different tobacco control efforts (Australia).

Substantial evidence from a broad range of studies supports the inclusion of graphic pictorial images on tobacco warning labels, as called for under the strong Article 11 Guidelines.
Graphic pictures can significantly enhance the effectiveness of
warning labels. In many countries, the warning label is the only
sustained population-level mechanism by which governments
inform their people about the harms of cigarettes and other tobacco products and, in those countries, the evidence-based inclusion of pictures could potentially lead to greater impact. For
decades, the tobacco industry has taken advantage of the package as a venue for creating positive associations for their product.

The use of graphic pictures is an important means of replacing those positive associations with negative associations, which is far more appropriate given the devastating impact of tobacco products on global health.

| *"In the present research, we hypothesize that warning messages may have different effects on smoking attitudes."*

Adding More Graphic Warnings to Cigarette Packs Will Backfire

Jochim Hansen, Susanne Winzeler, and Sascha Topolinski

Jochim Hansen is a professor of psychology at New York University, Susanne Winzeler is a professor of psychology at the University of Basel in Switzerland, and Sascha Topolinski is a professor of psychology at the University of Wurzburg in Germany. In the following viewpoint, the authors describe the findings of a study that suggests applying more graphic death-related warnings and imagery on cigarette packs may only make the products more attractive to younger smokers. According to the study results, many smokers in their teens and twenties smoke partly out of a sense of "devil-may-care" nihilism or rebelliousness, and for them warnings regarding their mortality would be construed as proof of their daring. The more iconic the death imagery adorning the packaging of their favored vice, the more their self-esteem would be reinforced.

Jochim Hansen, Susanne Winzeler, and Sascha Topolinski, "When the Death Makes You Smoke: A Terror Management Perspective on the Effectiveness of Cigarette On-Pack Warnings," *Journal of Experimental Social Psychology*, September 11, 2009, pp. 226–228. Copyright © 2009 by Elsevier Science Publishers. All rights reserved. Reproduced by permission.

As you read, consider the following questions:

1. According to the authors, what is the "terror management" health model and how does it apply to tobacco products?
2. What, in the authors' view, would be a more effective type of warning message targeting youth smokers?
3. On what two factors did the authors conclude the impact of warning messages on cigarette packs depend?

Smoking is responsible for millions of deaths all over the world and the figure is estimated to continue to rise. In an effort to help to reduce the number of tobacco consumers, governments started several anti-smoking strategies, such as raising the taxation on tobacco products, publicizing anti-smoking advertisements, or making certain public places smoke-free.

Labeling of tobacco products is yet another anti-smoking strategy. In many countries, every tobacco product has to have a message printed on the package that warns against the negative consequences of smoking for one's health. Such warnings shall make consumers aware that smoking leads to death (e.g., "Smoking kills") to health problems (e.g., "Smoking clogs the articles and causes heart attacks and strokes"), and to social problems (e.g., "Protect children: Do not make them breath your smoke"). Thereby, many of such warning messages remind us of our mortality, but others do not (e.g., "Smoking makes your skin age quicker"). How effective are such warnings in reducing smoking attitudes?

In the present research, we hypothesize that warning messages may have different effects on smoking attitudes, depending on (1) how salient mortality is in the messages, and on (2) how strongly recipients base their self-esteem on smoking. Specifically, we propose that, on the one hand, terrifying but death-unrelated warnings (such as "Smoking brings you and the people around you severe damage" and "Smoking makes you unattractive") are effective in reducing attitudes towards smoking to a greater degree the more people base their self-esteem on smoking. This is because such warnings may challenge the very reason for smoking particularly for those who believe that smoking allows them to feel valued by others or to boost their positive self-image. Thus, a high smoking-based self-esteem may make people especially susceptible for information that undermines their self-esteem.

The Terror Management Paradox

Based on the terror management health model, we predict on the other hand that the opposite pattern would emerge when the warnings are related to death and therefore make mortality salient. That is, the more individuals base their self-esteem on smoking, the more they would adopt a positive attitude towards smoking after being provided with mortality-salient warning messages because awareness of mortality motivates self-esteem striving. This hypothesis can be derived from terror management theory, which is based on the notion that all human beings are aware that their own death is inevitable. This knowledge creates the potential for extreme anxiety (or terror) because of being helplessly exposed to this threat. In order to manage this distress, people are motivated to maintain faith in their cultural worldview and to keep a positive self-esteem (i.e., they are motivated to increase the subjective belief that one is a valuable member of one's culture). Keeping a positive self-esteem can give a feeling of security and function to buffer people from the deeply rooted existential fear when mortality is made salient. To the extent that smoking is a source of self-esteem, mortality-salient on-pack warnings would thus ironically cause more positive attitudes towards smoking.

A comparable example for the buffer function of self-esteem has been shown by an experiment that examined the effects of mortality salience on risk taking while driving. Mortality salience inductions led to more risky driving than the control condition among individuals who perceived driving as relevant to their self-esteem. Similarly, it has been demonstrated that women for whom their looks were an important source of self-esteem preferred to eat fruit salad (compared to chocolate cake) if mortality was salient, whereas women who based their self-esteem on other things showed the opposite pattern.

In the present research, we assessed smoking-based self-esteem and afterwards presented smokers with fear-evoking warning messages on cigarette packages. These warnings were either related to death or not. After a delay, we measured smoking attitudes. We included a delay because any effects of mortality threats can only be found when death-related thoughts have been removed from conscious awareness, either by delay, by distraction, or by subliminal presentation of the mortality threats. When thoughts of death are in focal attention, behavior is guided by a motivation to overcome these thoughts. Only after thoughts of death have become nonconscious, motivations to bolster one's self-esteem may override such proximal defenses.

Because reminders of one's mortality may lead to attempts to bolster one's self-esteem in response to an existential threat, we predicted that mortality salience would paradoxically cause more positive smoking attitudes for individuals who build their self-esteem on smoking. Therefore, death-related anti-smoking warnings should be less effective in changing smoking attitudes the more people base their self-esteem on smoking. In contrast, death-neutral [but self-esteem related] anti-smoking warnings should more effectively induce anti-smoking attitudes the more smoking is a source of self-esteem. . . .

Death as a Selling Point

The present findings suggest that warning messages on cigarette packages can be effective in inducing anti-smoking attitudes. However, their effect depends on a combination of smoking-based self-esteem and mortality salience of the message. On the one hand, death-related warnings were not effective and even

ironically caused more positive smoking attitudes among tobacco consumers who based their self-esteem on smoking. This
finding suggests that individuals with a high smoking self-esteem
use positive smoking attitudes as a strategy to buffer against existential fears provoked by the death-related warning messages.
For individuals with a low smoking self-esteem, in contrast, a
positive attitude towards smoking would not buffer against existential terror. Thus, relative to high smoking self-esteem participants, participants with a low self-esteem demonstrated lower
smoking attitudes.

On the other hand, warning messages that were unrelated
to death effectively reduced smoking attitudes the more recipients based their self-esteem on smoking. This finding can be explained by the fact that the warnings such as "Smoking brings
you and the people around you severe damage" and "Smoking
makes you unattractive" may be particularly threatening to
people who believe the opposite, namely that smoking allows
them to feel valued by others to boost their positive self-image.
To the degree that warning messages undermine the high smoking-based self-esteem, smoking may be devalued. Interestingly,
this effect, too, only emerges when attitudes are assessed after a
delay but not when attitudes are assessed directly after the warning. Possibly, when smokers are consciously aware of warnings
that argue against the basis of their self-esteem, such warnings
may be downplayed. After a delay, however, the warnings are not
in conscious awareness anymore and may unfold their impacts.

In sum, consistent with the terror management theory and
the terror management health model, the impact of warning
messages on cigarette packages depended (1) on the degree to
which self-esteem was based on smoking, and (2) on the salience
of death in the warnings. Our finding is of high practical relevance, as it suggests that a differential strategy should be applied
to warn smokers against negative consequences of smoking, depending on the degree to which they base their self-esteem on
smoking. Death-related warnings are not effective and even have

unwanted effects when smokers have a high smoking-based self-esteem.

However, outside the laboratory, the degree to which smokers base their self-esteem on smoking is unknown. Thus, it is difficult to predict whether a death-related or a death-unrelated warning messages would be more effective. Yet, one could speculate that certain populations base their self-esteem on smoking to a higher degree than others, for instance young smokers who want to impress their peers. If this turns out to be true, a consequence of our findings would be that such populations should be warned against noxious consequences of smoking with death-neutral messages that undermine their smoking-based self-esteem. Such messages would probably not increase smoking attitudes as a strategy to buffer against existential fears, but instead change people's minds after a delay.

In general, when smokers are faced with death-related anti-smoking messages on cigarette packs, they produce active coping attempts as reflected in their willingness to continue the risky smoking behavior. Which coping attempts they use depends on their smoking-based self-esteem. To succeed with anti-smoking messages on cigarette packs one thus has to take into account that considering their death may make people smoke.

> "Regulating commercial speech for
> lawful products only because those
> products are widely disliked—even for
> cause—sets us on the path of regulating
> such speech for other products that may
> only be disfavored by a select few."

Banning Tobacco Ads
Is a Violation of the
First Amendment

Caroline Fredrickson and Michael Macleod-Ball

*Caroline Fredrickson is currently the executive director of the
American Constitution Society for Law and Policy (ACS). Michael
Macleod-Ball is the legislative chief of staff at the American Civil
Liberties Union (ACLU). The following viewpoint is a letter drafted
by Fredrickson and Macleod-Ball to the United States Senate regarding proposed restrictions on the banning of tobacco ads as part
of the Family Smoking Prevention and Tobacco Control Act signed
into law in 2009. In the letter, the authors state their concerns that
banning products, which some consider objectionable, is a slippery
slope and that advertising falls under the heading of free speech, an
inalienable constitutional right.*

As you read, consider the following questions:

1. What two objections are raised by the letter's authors with respect to the restrictive legislation under discussion?

2. According to the authors, what are some of the negative impacts that the restrictions on outdoor ads would have that they consider excessive?

3. On what grounds do the authors object to restricting tobacco ads more "than necessary," and do the statutes they are questioning seem in your view reasonable or unreasonable?

We are writing on behalf of the American Civil Liberties Union (ACLU) to express our concern over the advertising restrictions contained in S. 982, *The Family Smoking Prevention and Tobacco Control Act* (hereinafter the '2009 Tobacco Control Bill'). The ACLU is America's largest and oldest civil liberties organization, having over half a million members, countless additional activists and supporters, and 53 affiliates nationwide. We last commented on the issue of tobacco advertising regulation when S. 2626, the Youth Smoking Prevention and Public Health Protection Act of 2002 (hereinafter the '2002 Youth Smoking Bill'), was introduced during the 107th Congress. As in 2002, we continue to believe that the advertising restrictions in this year's bill are not drawn narrowly to achieve the stated public purpose and, as such, fail to comply with the free speech protections of the First Amendment. In the absence of a much more substantial narrowing of the advertising restrictions in a manner directly tied to the goal of reducing youth smoking, we urge the removal of the advertising restrictions set forth in Section 102 of the bill. It is our understanding that such an amendment is likely to be offered when the bill comes to the floor for consideration and we urge you to support it.

History

In 1995 the Food and Drug Administration (FDA) proposed regulations to restrict the sales and distribution of cigarettes and smokeless tobacco products to children and adolescents. In March of 2000, in *FDA v. Brown & Williamson Tobacco Corp.*, the Supreme Court ruled that Congress had not granted the FDA jurisdiction to regulate tobacco products as customarily marketed and the regulations were consequently revoked. The 2002 Youth Smoking Bill would have amended the Federal Food, Drug, and Cosmetic Act to give the Secretary of Health and Human Services (HHS) regulatory authority over tobacco products. In doing so the legislation would have codified the past restrictions (61 Fed. Reg. 44398, Aug. 28 1996). In the statement we submitted to the Senate Health, Education, Labor and Pensions Committee on September 18, 2002, we argued that:

1. The restrictions imposed by S. 2626 on advertising and other promotions of tobacco were inconsistent with the First Amendment; and

2. Restrictions on speech intended to reduce the number of children who begin smoking must be narrowly defined so as not to infringe on the rights of adults.

The 2009 Tobacco Control Bill would now impose most of the same restrictions as the 2002 Youth Smoking Bill. The only significant change impacting commercial speech restrictions is the acknowledgment of the ruling in *Lorillard Tobacco Co. v. Reilly*. In *Lorillard*, the Supreme Court struck down a state tobacco advertising regulation similar to the FDA's proposed rule. The Massachusetts regulation would have prohibited outdoor ads within 1,000 feet of schools, parks and playgrounds and also restricted point-of-sale advertising for tobacco products. Writing for the majority, Justice [Sandra Day] O'Connor found the Massachusetts regulation was not narrowly tailored enough to meet constitutional scrutiny. She also suggested the FDA regulation faced the same problem.

Section (102)(2)(E) of the 2009 Tobacco Control Bill responds to the *Lorillard* ruling by requiring new regulations to:

Include such modifications to section 897.30(b) [of 61 Fed. Reg. 44615-44618], if any, that the Secretary determines are appropriate in light of governing First Amendment case law, including the decision of the Supreme Court of the United States in *Lorillard Tobacco Co. v. Reilly*.

While we agree this is a step in the right direction, there is no affirmative adjustment to the prohibited restriction and only an implicit acknowledgement of the First Amendment implications of the ruling. Moreover, the remaining restrictions were left largely intact and we do not believe they are any more narrowly tailored to the public purpose of reducing youth smoking than the outdoor ad restriction addressed in *Lorillard*. The remaining restrictions would, among other things:

1. Restrict all advertising to black and white format;
2. Allow unrestricted advertising in only those publications which have an 85% or more adult readership, and fewer than 2 million youth readers;
3. Restrict labeling and advertising in an audio format to words without music, and limit video format to static black text on a white background;
4. Ban logo and brand names on race cars, driver uniforms, and the like;
5. Ban the use of tobacco brand names on non-tobacco products (e.g., t-shirts, caps, lighters);
6. Ban the use of tobacco brand names associated with non-tobacco products;
7. Ban brand-name event sponsorships; and
8. Ban distribution of free product samples, either in person or through the mail.

Under First Amendment analysis, any such speech limitation must be no more restrictive than necessary and must directly advance the government's objective in reducing smoking by youths.

In 2002, we noted that neither FDA studies nor legislative findings were sufficient to meet the *Liquormart* test.* Nothing in the 2009 record causes us to change our opinion in that regard. Regulating commercial speech for lawful products only because those products are widely disliked—even for cause—sets us on the path of regulating such speech for other products that may only be disfavored by a select few in a position to impose their personal preferences through misuse of the regulatory process. Instead, we suggest a determined application of the laws prohibiting false advertising and a continuation of the vigorous and successful efforts to warn the American public—including its children—of the harms associated with the use of tobacco products. Usually, the antidote to harmful speech can be found in the wisdom of countervailing speech—not in the outright ban of the speech perceived as harmful.

We urge you to support any amendment that would remove the advertising restrictions in Section 102 of S. 982.

Note

* In the 1996 case of *44 Liquormart, Inc. v. Rhode Island*, the Supreme Court ruled that the state's ban on the advertising of liquor prices violated the First Amendment's free speech provision.

> "There is something to be said about our value system here, because tobacco products challenge everything about it."

Tobacco Ads Endanger Women

Anna Quindlen

Anna Quindlen is the author of five best-selling books and a regular columnist for Newsweek. *In the following viewpoint, Quindlen discusses how tobacco companies have started targeting women with their advertisements—specifically, the product Camel No. 9. The product uses pink and teal accents with a tiny pink camel to appeal more to women and entice them to smoke. She argues that tobacco companies buy ads specifically targeted towards women in an attempt to manipulate the consumers into endangering their health.*

As you read, consider the following questions:

1. According to the author, how do tobacco companies target women?
2. What did more than three dozen House members ask magazines with larger female readerships to do?

In a world of uncertainty, there's always one group you can count on: the tobacco industry. Their executives aren't quite as riveting as they were years ago, when they were the last people in America swearing there was no link between cigarettes and cancer. Now they sponsor stop-smoking sites and cultural events to play the corporate solid citizen, but they're still selling the same old thing—yellow teeth, smelly upholstery, wrinkles, emphysema, lung cancer and death. To do this they need to think outside the box. Especially since the box is a coffin.

Most recently R.J. Reynolds, the firm that insisted that just because Joe Camel was a cartoon character didn't mean he was supposed to appeal to kids, have come up with a new product called Camel No. 9. It's a cigarette for women—decorative pink band, teeny pink camel, ebony box with hot-pink and teal accents. Of course when a cigarette is for women, it's really for girls; since lung cancer has now outstripped breast cancer as the leading cancer killer of women, younger smokers have to be constantly created to fill the death gap. About 90 percent of all smokers begin before age 18, according to the Centers for Disease Control, and, as my favorite 18-year-old reports from college, Camel No. 9 may be the perfect gateway cigarette for the younger set. "That perfumery smell," she reports, "translates into this almost lovely aftertaste that I've always placed as a very, very light hint of caramel and chai tea." Lyrical, huh? She could write copy for a tobacco company if she didn't know her mother would lock her out of the house.

Maybe it was the pink-foil package lining, or the slogan "light and luscious," but anti-tobacco advocacy organizations jumped right on Camel No. 9, and before you could say "chemo," 45 groups ranging from the Coalition of Labor Union Women to the American Academy of Pediatrics were demanding that R.J. Reynolds pull it from the market. Some members of Congress decided to ask women's magazines to lead the way. "I commend them for the role they've taken in women's health," said Congresswoman Lois Capps, a nurse from California. Capps knew that there were some magazines that had long ago decided not to accept cigarette ads. "*Good Housekeeping* didn't get hooked on the dollars," said Ellen Levine, the former editor of the magazine, which hasn't run cigarette ads since 1952.

Well-Known Movie Stars Once Advertised for Cigarette Brands

Big movie stars were happy to endorse smokes on TV [in the 1950s and 1960s], and the number one celebrity of the era was the Duke. John Wayne appeared for Camel in 1952, speaking highly of the product: "Mild and good tasting pack after pack. And I know, I've been smokin' 'em for twenty years." . . .

Coincidentally (or not), John Wayne died of lung cancer twenty-seven years after that spot aired; some of the last commercials he filmed were to ask people to *stop* smoking.

Billy Ingram, "Lighten Up & Light Up (or vice versa)," www.tvparty.com.

So more than three dozen House members wrote to 11 magazines with large female readerships, asking them to voluntarily stop accepting ads for Camel No. 9. The silence was deafening, which the signatories found surprising; usually when Congress calls, people respond. After a second letter, a few editors replied, but none agreed to stop running the ads. The publisher of *Vogue* even sent back a huffy reply that made it sound as though asking a fashion magazine not to run cigarette ads was like asking *The New York Times* not to run the Pentagon Papers. "At odds with the basic fabric of our country's value system," was one phrase.

There is something to be said about our value system here, because tobacco products challenge everything about it. Congress is considering a bill to give the Food and Drug Administration [FDA] more power over how cigarettes are advertised, distributed and manufactured, but all those involved pull back from the logical endgame, which is to have the FDA fully regulate them. That's because if it did, it would have to ban cigarettes, which have no useful purpose and commonly lead to addiction, illness and death. But the industry is a powerful economic and lobbying force, millions are already addicted and Americans naturally recoil from prohibition. The result is this constant dance around the dissemination of a legal, lethal drug delivery system.

Representatives of R.J. Reynolds insist, as they always do, that they are not trying to garner new smokers with Camel No. 9, cute and cool as the product may appear to teenagers. They say they seek only to shift existing smokers to a new brand. Mathematically this is preposterous. An estimated 438,000 deaths annually, or one in five in this country, are due to smoking. Smokers die more than a decade earlier than nonsmokers. The windfall for cigarette manufacturers is that somewhere near a hospital there's always a high school.

So, like Congresswoman Capps, those who care about the health of young women do not look to the tobacco industry. It's no wonder that they looked to American magazines, often a key source on information about diet, exercise, child rearing and medical issues. But there has been a dissonance between editorial and ads. *Newsweek*, for example, publishes frequent service pieces about women's health, but also accepted ads for Camel No. 9. Most editors will say that they don't run many cigarette ads anyhow, but that raises the question of why they need to run any at all. Cigarette manufacturers have the right to try to buy ad space, and to manipulate consumers in order to sell their product. They have a compact with the bottom line. But magazines have a compact with their readers. And that means not only writing about products that will kill them, but forgoing ads for those products as well.

Periodical and Internet Sources Bibliography

The following articles have been selected to supplement the diverse views presented in this chapter.

Debby Berlyne	"Smoking in Movies and Television," *Robert Wood Johnson Foundation Retrospective Series*, April 2011.
Walter Brasch	"Questions Remain in Government's Anti-Cigarette Campaign," *The Moderate Voice*, June 23, 2011.
Christopher Caldwell	"Smoking Ads Are More About Class than Compassion," *Financial Times*, June 24, 2011.
Serena Gordon	"Teen Girls Say Pink Camel in Cigarette Ads Caught Their Eye," *Bloomberg Businessweek*, March 15, 2010.
Reiner Hanewinkel	"Cigarette Smoking and Perception of a Movie Character in a Film Trailer," *Arch Pediatric Adolescent Medicine*, vol. 163, no. 1, January 2009, pp. 15–18.
Kim Masters	"Puff Piece: Harvard Tells Hollywood to Ban Cigarettes from Kids' Movies," *Slate*, April 6, 2007.
Marina Picciotto	"Smoking in Movies: Why Your Brain Thinks It's Cool," *Huffington Post*, January 19, 2011.
Josh Rottenberg	"CDC to Hollywood: Stop with the Smoking Already!" *Entertainment Weekly*, August 19, 2010.
Stephen Smith	"Tobacco Signs Still Target City's Poorer Areas," *Boston Globe*, August 23, 2010, pp. 136–142.
Stanford University Medical Center	"Point-of-Sale Advertising Major Cause of Teen Smoking, Study Shows," *ScienceDaily*, July 19, 2010.

For Further Discussion

Chapter 1

1. The Centers for Disease Control and Prevention researchers note that global tobacco use over the past decade is on the rise, especially among the poor. Marc Kaufman, however, claims other figures suggest that smoking rates have been in steady decline if the study is expanded to describe the world population since 1951. Assuming all statistics referenced in both articles are correct, which of these viewpoints do you believe is more persuasive and why?

2. While Richa Gulati believes that teenage social smokers are especially vulnerable to chemical dependencies, Ray Hainer claims that the addiction is psychological in origin. On what points, if any, do the authors seem to agree and which author makes a better case for her or his position?

3. Based on their study, Mattias Oberg, Maritta S. Jaakkola, Alistair Woodward, Armando Peruga, and Annette Pruss-Ustun believe that the health consequences of secondhand smoke have been vastly underreported and constitute a global epidemic. However, Michael Siegel says that all research on secondhand smoke is tainted by inaccuracies such as the one he cites from another study, which claims that secondhand smoke is as deadly as the vapor inhaled directly by smokers. Taking Siegel's interpretation at face value, do you feel his argument invalidates the conclusions reached by the authors of the opposing viewpoint? Why or why not?

Chapter 2

1. Editors for the organization Action on Smoking and Health (ASH) believe that smoking bans in public places are effective deterrents by reinforcing the notion that smoking is socially unacceptable. Yet, Thomas A. Lambert asserts that

smoking bans only serve to make smoking appear more tantalizing, a forbidden fruit that will only tempt impressionable youths eager to flaunt their sense of rebellion. Which argument do you agree with and why?

2. Amartya Sen contends that smoking bans should be mandatory because the victims of smoking include not only every nonsmoker on earth, including millions of children, but also the smokers themselves. Jacob Sullum argues that smoking bans are infringements of human liberty and misguided efforts to impose behavior patterns on the basis of hypothetical virtue rather than measurable health statistics. Based on their arguments, who do you most agree with? Are smoking bans fair or unfair? Use supporting or opposing arguments from the viewpoints to supplement your position.

3. What are "sin taxes" and what reasons do Rachel Kaprielian and Herman Hamilton furnish to support their conviction that imposing them is justified? What do you think Bruce Smith and Kathryn Hickok consider the injustice of sin taxes? Who do you believe makes a more compelling argument for or against sin taxes?

4. Prabhat Jha says that curbing worldwide tobacco use is a moral imperative, while Tony Newman asserts that restricting access to tobacco would simply drive the business underground and ultimately cause more harm than mere inaction. How does it appear that each author estimated harm and suffering? What factors did they consider or overlook? Explain.

Chapter 3

1. Prue Talbot and Anna Trtchounian believe that electronic cigarettes should be regulated and require further study before being approved as smoking-cessation aids. However, Michael Siegel argues that by definition e-cigarettes represent a safer alternative, as liquid heated by electricity is

a cleaner delivery method than inhaling burnt vegetable matter. Whose viewpoint do you believe is better supported and why?

2. Do you think that the members of the Center for Tobacco Products make a persuasive case for exempting menthols from their proposed ban of flavored cigarettes? Based on her viewpoint, would Elizabeth Nolan Brown endorse or decry a ban of menthol cigarettes that were not manufactured in America?

3. Both the viewpoint by Lorinda Bullock and the one by Jeff Stier and Brad Rodu reference the same Swedish study on smokeless tobacco. While Bullock contends that the study reinforces her claims that chewing tobacco and snuff have risen in popularity among young men, Stier and Rodu claim that this should be cause for celebration, as it signifies a corresponding national decline in traditional smoking. Which viewpoint do you agree or disagree with? On what basis do you believe that the use of smoking alternatives should be encouraged, if at all?

Chapter 4

1. What reasons do the researchers at the National Cancer Institute provide for their assertion that all movies featuring a character smoking should automatically receive an "R" rating? What reasons does Simon Chapman give for his conclusion that doing so would be pointless as a deterrent and irreparably coarsen the art form? Do you agree or disagree with each author? Which viewpoint do you believe is better supported and why?

2. Geoffrey T. Fong, David Hammond, and Sara C. Hitchman say that the addition of grislier graphic warnings on cigarette packs would be a particularly effective deterrent in countries with lower literacy rates. Yet, Jochim Hansen, Susanne Winzeler, and Sascha Topolinski note that younger smokers

in all countries tend to respond with defiance to graphic symbols of death, as opposed to sterile written warnings that they disregard altogether. In their view, the placement of such warnings would backfire and even raise smoking rates. Which viewpoint do you agree with? Explain.

3. Do you think that the ACLU's Caroline Fredrickson and Michael Macleod-Ball make a compelling argument that outdoor tobacco advertising is a form of free speech? What restrictions on tobacco advertising do you feel should be enforced, if any, and why?

Organizations to Contact

The editors have compiled the following list of organizations concerned with the issues debated in this book. The descriptions are derived from materials provided by the organizations. All have publications or information available for interested readers. The list was compiled on the date of publication of the present volume; names, addresses, phone and fax numbers, and e-mail and Internet addresses may change. Be aware that many organizations take several weeks or longer to respond to inquiries, so allow as much time as possible.

American Cancer Society
901 E Street NW, Suite 500
Washington, DC 20004
(800) 227-2345
website: www.cancer.org

The aim of the American Cancer Society (ACS) is the elimination of cancer through research, advocacy, and service. The organization works in conjunction with national partners to legislate for and implement comprehensive tobacco control programs. The ACS advocates social and environmental changes at the national, state, and community levels to prevent young people from taking up tobacco and furnishes support for those who wish to stop smoking. The ACS website includes tobacco-related resources on topics such as smoking, the health consequences of tobacco, and updates on the international tobacco control movement.

American Council on Science and Health
1995 Broadway, 2nd Floor
New York, NY 10023-5860
(212) 362-7044 • fax: (212) 362-4919
e-mail: acsh@acsh.org
website: www.acsh.org

The American Council on Science and Health (ACSH) is a nonprofit consumer education consortium concerned with the scientific justification for imposing national policies related to public health and the environment. The group publishes editorials, position analyses, and books on a variety of health issues. Tobacco use is one of nine topics specifically addressed on the organization's website.

American Lung Association

61 Broadway, 6th Floor
New York, NY 10006
(212) 315-8700
website: www.lungusa.org

The American Lung Association (ALA) is a publicly funded non-profit organization concerned with the causes of lung disease, including tobacco use, as well as prevention of the disease. Its website features articles on research and treatment of lung-related ailments and an extensive section on tobacco control.

Campaign for Tobacco Free Kids

1400 Eye Street, Suite 1200
Washington, DC 20005
(202) 296-5469
website: www.tobaccofreekids.org

The principal aim of the Campaign for Tobacco Free Kids is to shift public attitudes and policy on tobacco use by educating the public as well as policy makers about tobacco, exposing the industry's efforts to market tobacco to children, advocating methods to reduce tobacco use and exposure to secondhand smoke, and mobilizing organizations and individuals to lobby against its use. The group's website includes myriad special reports on issues ranging from smokeless tobacco concerns and tobacco-free campuses to ways in which tobacco consumption is influenced by products that contain nicotine.

Cato Institute
1000 Massachusetts Ave. NW
Washington, DC 20001-5403
(202) 842-0200 • fax: (202) 842-3490
e-mail: cato@cato.org
website: www.cato.org

The Cato Institute is a libertarian public policy research foundation devoted to limiting the role of government and protecting
individual rights. The group opposes most forms of government
regulation in general. The institute's website offers a miscellany
of editorial commentaries and policy papers concerning the tobacco industry and aspects of the regulatory environment.

Competitive Enterprise Institute
1001 Connecticut Ave. NW
Washington, DC 20036
(202) 331-1010 • fax: (202) 331-0640
website: www.cei.org

The Competitive Enterprise Institute (CEI) is a nonprofit public policy organization dedicated to promoting the principles
of free enterprise and limited government mandates. It believes
that individuals are best helped not by federal intervention but
by making their own choices in a free marketplace. CEI opposes
any government role in the regulation of tobacco products and
staunchly supports individual choice. Archived on its site are
opinion pieces and essays, mostly involving (and denouncing)
issues of government regulation of tobacco products.

Heartland Institute
19 South LaSalle Street, Suite 903
Chicago, IL 60603
(312) 377-4000
e-mail: think@heartland.org
website: www.heartland.org

The agenda of the Heartland Institute is to discover, develop, and promote free market remedies to social and economic problems. Such remedies include market-based approaches to environmental protection, privatization of public services, choice and personal responsibility in health care, and mass deregulation in areas it claims are better controlled by property rights and markets. The Heartland Institute website features a number of documents dealing with state tobacco taxation, the federal regulation of tobacco products, and the harm-reduction concept.

National Center on Addiction and Substance Abuse at Columbia University
633 Third Ave., 19th Floor
New York, NY 10017-6706
(212) 841-5200
website: www.casacolumbia.org

Founded in 1992 by former US secretary of health, education and welfare Joseph A. Califano, Jr., the National Center on Addiction and Substance Abuse at Columbia University (CASA) has as its mission to inform Americans of the social and economic costs of substance abuse and its impact on their lives, as well as to help diminish the stigma of substance abuse. CASA, whose staff is composed of specialists in the medical, social science, and legal fields, studies and lobbies against abuse of all toxic substances—nicotine and alcohol, as well as illegal, prescription, and performance enhancing drugs—throughout all strata of society.

National Institute on Drug Abuse
6001 Executive Blvd.
Bethesda, MD 20892
website: www.nida.nih.gov

The National Institute on Drug Abuse (NIDA) is a branch of the National Institutes of Health. NIDA's mission is to use scientific methods to fight drug abuse and addiction. It endorses and conducts research across a wide range of scientific disciplines and disseminates the results to improve prevention, treatment, and public policy with regard to drug addiction, including tobacco addiction. The NIDA website features materials on nicotine addiction for students and youths.

Office of the Surgeon General
5600 Fishers Lane, Room 18-66
Rockville, MD 20857
(301) 443-4000
website: www.surgeongeneral.gov

The surgeon general is the United States' chief health educator. He or she serves to provide the most accurate and current scientific information available on how to improve health and reduce the risk of illness or injury. The website of the surgeon general's office features an array of resources related to tobacco use reduction, including detailed resources on smoking and cancer, the effects of exposure to tobacco smoke, the Federal Cigarette and Labeling Act, and numerous materials on how to quit smoking.

US Food and Drug Administration
5600 Fishers Lane
Rockville, MD 20857-0001
(888) 463-6332
website: www.fda.gov

The US Food and Drug Administration (FDA) is responsible for protecting the health of the public by ensuring the safety, efficacy, and security of human and veterinary drugs, medical devices, biological products and services, the nation's food supply, cosmetics, and products that emit radiation or other toxic substances. The FDA's mandate also includes advancing the public health by helping to improve innovations that make medicine and food safer and more affordable, and by disseminating accurate, science-based medical and nutritional information. As the result of a 2001 US Supreme Court ruling that the agency lacks the authority to regulate tobacco, the FDA website does not contain materials related specifically to tobacco but does furnish a link to www.smokefree.gov, which offers extensive information on how to quit smoking and the potential consequences of not quitting.

Bibliography of Books

Ann A. Abbott

Alcohol, Tobacco, and Other Drugs: Challenging Myths, Assessing Theories, Individualizing Interventions. Washington, DC: NASW Press, 2010.

Jason Aaron Baca

Nicotine Rage: A Guide to Quitting Chewing Tobacco. College Station, TX: Virtualbookworm.com Publishing, 2009.

Peter Bearman, Kathryn M. Neckerman, and Leslie Wright, eds.

After Tobacco: What Would Happen If Americans Stopped Smoking? New York: Columbia University Press, 2011.

Kirsten Bell, Darlene McNaughton, and Amy Salmon, eds.

Alcohol, Tobacco and Obesity: Morality, Mortality and the New Public Health. London, U.K.: Routledge, 2011.

Peter Benson

Tobacco Capitalism: Growers, Migrant Workers, and the Changing Face of a Global Industry. Princeton: Princeton University Press, 2011.

E.R. Billings

Tobacco: Its History, Varieties, Culture, Manufacture and Commerce. Memphis: General Books LLC, 2010.

Allan M. Brandt

The Cigarette Century: The Rise, Fall and Deadly Persistence of the Product That Defined America. New York: Basic Books, 2007.

Eric Burns — *The Smoke of the Gods: A Social History of Tobacco*. Philadelphia: Temple University Press, 2007.

Simon Chapman — *Public Health Advocacy and Tobacco Control: Making Smoking History*. Oxford: Wiley-Blackwell, 2007.

James Fitzgerald — *The Joys of Smoking Cigarettes*. New York: It Books, 2007.

A. Lee Fritschler and Catherine E. Rudder — *Smoking and Politics: Bureaucracy Centered Policymaking*. Upper Saddle River, NJ: Prentice Hall, 2006.

Donald G. Gifford — *Suing the Tobacco and Lead Pigment Industries: Government Litigation as Public Health Prescription*. Ann Arbor: University of Michigan Press, 2010.

Sander L. Gilman and Xun Zhou, eds. — *Smoke: A Global History of Smoking*. London, U.K.: Reaktion Books, 2004.

Arlene Hirschfelder — *Tobacco (Health and Medical Issues Today)*. Westport, CT: Greenwood, 2010.

Meyer Jacobstein — *The Tobacco Industry in the United States*. Charleston, SC: Nabu Press. 2010.

David Kessler — *A Question of Intent: A Great American Battle with a Deadly Industry*. New York: PublicAffairs, 2002.

Ann Malaspina

False Images, Deadly Promises: Smoking and the Media (Tobacco: The Deadly Drug). Broomall: Mason Crest, 2007.

Naomi Oreskes and Erik M. Conway

Merchants of Doubt: How a Handful of Scientists Obscured the Truth on Issues from Tobacco Smoke to Global Warming. New York: Bloomsbury Press, 2011.

Robert L. Rabin and Stephen D. Sugarman, eds.

Regulating Tobacco. Oxford: Oxford University Press, 2001.

Juliann Sivulka

Soap, Sex, and Cigarettes: A Cultural History of American Advertising. Florence, KY: Wadsworth Publishing, 2011.

Clete Snell

Peddling Poison: The Tobacco Industry and Kids. Westport, CT: Praeger, 2005.

Judy Vaknin

Smoke Signals: 100 Years of Tobacco Advertising. Oxfordshire, U.K.: Libri Publishing, 2007.

William Wesley Young

The Story of the Cigarette. Ebookgalaxy, 2011.

Index